Thomas Hill: The Grand View

Marjorie Dakin Arkelian
Preface by George W. Neubert

The Oakland Museum Art Department
Oakland, California 1980

Cover Illustration: YOSEMITE VALLEY (El Capitan and Bridal Veil Fall)
88 × 72 in.
Collection of The Oakland Museum
Bequest of Dr. Cecil E. Nixon.

Exhibition Itinerary

The Oakland Museum
September 23–November 16, 1980

Tacoma Art Museum, Tacoma, Washington
March 4–April 13, 1981

Joslyn Art Museum, Omaha, Nebraska
May 9–June 21, 1981

Anchorage Historical and Fine Arts Museum,
Anchorage, Alaska
July 15–August 31, 1981

The Midland Art Council of the Midland Center for
the Arts, Inc., Midland, Michigan
September–October, 1981

This project is supported by a grant from the National
Endowment for the Arts, Washington, D.C., a Federal agency.

Biography by Marjorie Dakin Arkelian
Preface by George W. Neubert
Catalogue compiled by Barbara Bowman
Graphic Design by Jonathan Hirabayashi
Photography by Joe Samberg
Offset Lithography and Color Separations by Cal Central Press,
    Sacramento, California
Typesetting by Design & Type, Inc., San Francisco, California
Bookbinding by Cardoza-James, San Francisco, California

Fig. 1:   EMERALD BAY, LAKE TAHOE, 1883
          27 × 45 in.
          Collection of the Los Angeles County Museum of Art
          Gift of Mr. and Mrs. Robert B. Honeyman, Jr.

With Gratitude

The Oakland Museum is especially indebted to John H. Garzoli for his generous gift which enabled the Art Department to match its grant from the National Endowment for the Arts for this exhibition and catalogue.

In light of his enthusiastic involvement with American art, it seems appropriate that he is the patron for this exhibition, *Thomas Hill: The Grand View*. A native of San Francisco, he grew up in an environment of fine art—his father was an art collector and his great-uncle was the California artist Giuseppe Cadenasso. During his twenty years as a dealer specializing in nineteenth and twentieth-century American art, John Garzoli has also developed an outstanding personal collection of the art of California.

It is with gratitude that we accept the support of John H. Garzoli, who for years has recognized and understood the vision and facility of Thomas Hill.

Contents

Acknowledgments

Much credit for the presentation of this exhibition is due to individuals and institutions who provided invaluable sources and assistance. All participants cannot be named; however, special mentions include the following persons: Martha Shipman Andrews; Theodore Baggelmann; James H. Brown; Ward Childs; Madeleine Ann Darcy; Lawrence Dinnean; William C. Frost; John H. Garzoli; Abigail Booth Gerdts; William H. Gerdts; Phyllis F. Greene; Robin Hamlyn; Richard R. Hanna; Ann Harlow; James D. Hart; Wawona Washburn Hartwig; Ethel Hill; F. Herbert and Margaret Hoover; Jack Jackson; Howard and Beryl Lea; Dorothy McCullough Lee; Maud Lindemann; Ronald Lindbaugh; Betty Hoag McGlynn; L.K. Morey; Paul C. Mills; Harry Mulford; Roxanne Nilan; Carol Osborne; Christine Reid; Shirley Sargent; Harold Settlemier; Robert L. Shalkop; Charles C. and Betty Smith; Charles Thrower; Charles and Gloria Vogel; Robert C. Vose, Jr.; Catherine Ward; and Richard V. West.

We are deeply grateful to the following institutions: Ann Bremer Memorial Library of the San Francisco Art Institute; Archives of American Art, San Francisco office; The Bancroft Library and The Doe Library of the University of California; Boston Athenaeum; Boston Public Library; California State Library; California Historical Society; The Fine Arts Museums of San Francisco; Frick Art Reference Library; Haverhill Public Library; Hirschl & Adler, Inc.; Holt-Atherton Pacific Center for Western Studies; Kennedy Galleries, Inc.; Leland Stanford, Jr. Art Museum and Archives; Levi-Heywood Memorial Library; The Metropolitan Museum of Art; M.H. de Young Memorial Museum and Library; Madera County Historical Society; Maxwell Galleries, Ltd.; The National Collection of Fine Arts, Smithsonian Institution; New Hampshire Historical Society; New York University; The New-York Historical Society; The Sierra Club; The Tate Gallery; Wells Fargo Bank History Room; and Yosemite National Park Research Center.

The cooperation of the Art Department staff of The Oakland Museum was indispensable. Barbara Bowman contributed in every aspect including research and compilation of the catalogue listings and bibliography. Harvey L. Jones assumed heavy responsibilities. He and Theodore Cohen, assisted by Gary Lopez, superintended the installation of the show. Therese Thau Heyman provided perceptive suggestions and advice. Odette Mayers, Leonard Walton, and Valliere Richard assisted with research. Carol Rosset expedited arrangements for the transportation of paintings. Jonathan Hirabayashi provided the graphic design for the catalogue.

We also extend our appreciation to the lenders to the show: to the Art Guild for their additional support for the catalogue; to the Womens' Board of the Oakland Museum Association; and to the members of the Volunteer Art Research Committee. These contributors are listed separately.

We are especially grateful to the National Endowment for the Arts, a Federal Agency, for providing a generous grant toward the exhibition and catalogue.

Marjorie Dakin Arkelian
Art Historian Emeritus

George W. Neubert
Curator of the Exhibition

Preface

This retrospective exhibition, *Thomas Hill: The Grand View*, provides an appropriate opportunity to reassess the significance of one of the most prolific painters of picturesque California scenes. This exhibition, within necessary limitations, traces Thomas Hill's stylistic development while documenting his expressive versatility and establishing his personal contribution to the tradition of landscape as subject in American art.

Earlier, numerous Eastern painters of the grandiloquent landscape had pictorially raided the far West for its unusual and expansive scenery. But, for the most part, these Hudson River landscape painters merely applied a preconceived formula and technique while trying to capture the drama of this region's natural wonders.

Working a decade or so later, Thomas Hill was a transitional figure in American landscape painting, synthesizing the influences of his German-trained teacher in Paris and that of the Barbizon painters. Hill formulated his own spontaneous and forceful style of painting to match the immensity of the inspiration and spectacular views of California and the West. Compared to the studio-conceived exaggerated canvases of many of his peers, the paintings of Thomas Hill are more expressive in capturing the majestic views of the far West.

Utilizing his traditional training and strong compositional structure, Thomas Hill in his mature work arranges repeated forms across the picture plane, managing light and atmosphere to keep the eye engaged throughout the panoramic stretch of nature while fusing a unified color system with loose painterly brush work where color floats free from descriptive form. This unique culmination of processes and techniques creates a native proto-impressionism predating many of the French Impressionist influences in American painting.

For Thomas Hill, the California landscape, and in particular Yosemite, provided an aesthetic vehicle for a set of formal visual inventions as a means of personal expression of his grand view.

George W. Neubert
Curator of the Exhibition

October 3.[10] Thomas Hill (tailor) found work in his trade in Syracuse, New York, but before he could send for his family, his wife, Maria, gave birth to a son, Edward Hill, on December 9, 1843, in the Wolverhampton poorhouse.[11] Edward, fourteen years younger than his brother Thomas, was also destined to become an American landscape painter.

The family letters reveal beyond doubt that Thomas Hill (artist), son of Thomas Hill (tailor), did not come to the United States in 1840 or 1841 as has been repeatedly documented. When his father was financially able to send for the family, Maria and her children sailed from Liverpool on July 8, 1844, aboard the *Queen of the West*. Although they traveled with the 275 steerage passengers, young Thomas was employed three weeks by the ship's cook and "of course lived well on everything fresh and had the chance of taking to his mother many things considered nice at sea." Ultimately, however, the only food left for crew and passengers alike was oatmeal. The thirty-eight-day voyage ended when the family was reunited in New York City on August 13, 1844.[12]

After borrowing three dollars from a friendly English tailor, father Thomas took his family aboard the steamboat *Providence* to Taunton, Massachusetts. Borrowing more money, he rented a house and found work as a tailor. He also consulted a designer in Taunton, Thomas Ben Hinton, about "a job for my boy, Tom." They "had a talk about the lad." Apparently, at this time, however, Hinton was unable to help Tom in his search for a job in the arts.[13]

On November 28, 1844, Thomas Hill (tailor) wrote to his brother Francis that "trade is good here," and mentioned that with the help of the two oldest boys family fortunes were improving. In February, 1845, he wrote to a friend:

> All the prices I have noted down are in English currency. Tom gets 5/6 a week and Frank 5/6; they work in the same cotton factory....All boys in this state must go to school three months out of the twelve while they are under fifteen...they have not told ours they must go to school yet.[14]

Although Thomas Hill (tailor), according to his letters, was an educated man, he was much more concerned at this time with contributions from his boys toward family support than for their further education.

Within a year, Tom had found work which was much more to his liking. His father wrote to brother Francis in Wolverhampton:

> Tom is working for a carriage painter and has been at it about 2 months....He gets 2-½ dollars a week and eats and sleeps at home....Tom would be glad if you would send him one ounce of carmine and ½ lb of Lake from Greens in Dudley Street and send word what it costs.[15]

"Tom gets on very creditably to himself and very profitable to me; he is never out of work and Frank is helping him now," wrote Thomas Hill (tailor) in 1847.[16] But the father's plan to depend on his son for financial support

Fig. 2: LAND'S END
15⅛ × 22 in.
Collection of The Oakland Museum
Gift of Grace Decker Meyer in memory of her husband,
Victorien Melville Meyer.

was dashed when Tom, who was recommended by his Taunton employers to a Boston firm of interior decorators, suddenly left home. When he returned in five weeks he was met with a cool reception which ended in an agreement between father and son. His father wrote:

> I compromised with him by selling him his liberty for 2 dollars a week till he is of age and he is to bear all expenses whatsoever. He gave me 20 dollars for the time he had been away...in general he wanted to handle his own earnings and to be his own master entirely and to make peace I did what I tell you.[17]

Tom continued successfully with the designing firm in Boston for two or three years. On September 2, 1851, his mother died at the age of forty-four in Chelsea, Massachusetts, where the family had made a new Home.[18] Two months later, on November 16, in Boston, Thomas Hill (artist), age twenty-two, married Charlotte Matilda Hawkes, a young woman of Scottish descent.[19]

Hill began to pursue his artistic career in earnest in 1853. In that year he moved with his wife and their first child to Philadelphia. His purpose was to attend the Pennsylvania Academy of the Fine Arts; however, to support his family he painted carriages in his spare time. Hill, now twenty-four, enrolled in the life class which was informally directed by the American-born landscape and portrait painter, Peter Frederick Rothermel.[20] Unfortunately, there are no extant records of the Academy from that period which might give further information concerning Hill's studies. During the 1850s there was no paid faculty or regular schedule of classes. Rather, instruction consisted of drawing from life and from antique casts and copying old master paintings from reproductions. Criticism and instruction were supplied by the more advanced students and by the Pennsylvania Academicians. Rothermel was a Pennsylvania Academician, first elected in 1847.[21]

Also in 1853, Hill was awarded a silver medal for a fruit and flower study sent to a Maryland Institute exhibition, "Promotion of the Mechanic Arts," in Baltimore. Membership in the old Graphic Club was included with the award.[22]

Hill, having made the final determination to make his living as a fine arts painter, continued to study informally at the Academy. In the summer of 1854, he engaged in landscape painting in the White Mountains of New Hampshire. He and artist Benjamin Champney became friends; Hill was the guest of Champney and his family in North Conway, New Hampshire, in 1854, and again in 1858.[23]

> Hill stayed at Champney's when he came alone. Otherwise he stayed at Thompson's, a small inn "where all the poor struggling artists stayed in the 1850s and 1860s. It was cheap. There also stayed Casilear, Kensett, Church, Fisher, Inness, Shapleigh, and E.W. Perry. All the above listed artists gave the Thompsons paintings for board and room."[24]

In the fall of 1855, Thomas Hill (artist) moved with his wife and three children to Cambridge, Massachusetts.

Fig. 3: FOUR HORSE HITCH, 1854
25 × 30¼ in.
Collection of the Shelburne Museum.

Fig. 4: *opposite page*
SUGAR LOAF PEAK, EL DORADO COUNTY, 1865
40 × 54 in.
Collection of the Crocker Art Museum.

There he was close to his Hill family relatives and to the New England countryside he loved to paint. Tragedy struck, however, when two of his children, Thomas, Jr. and Agnes died of diphtheria.[25]

Hill was active in Boston art circles. He became a regular member of the artists' group now known as "The White Mountain School" of landscapists, which included Champney, Asher B. Durand, George Inness, Albert Bierstadt, Virgil Williams—who was to become his lifetime friend in California—and many others.[26]

In his memorable book about life with his fellow artists in New England, Champney wrote:

> Thomas Hill has all the faculties of Bierstadt, and can make more pictures in a given time than any man I have ever met. In one afternoon of 3 hours in the White Mountain forests I have seen him produce a study, 12 × 20 in size, full of detail and brilliant light. There is his great strength, and his White Mountain wood interiors have not been excelled.[27]

Perhaps Champney's undated remarks about his friend refer to a later period when they painted together again in the late 1860s and early 1870s. Certainly, the few known oil paintings by Hill from the 1850s do not resemble his mature individualized style and techniques. *Four Horse Hitch*, 1854 (The Shelburne Museum), a rare and original New England scene, which other than family portraits is perhaps Hill's earliest known oil painting, bears the stamp of the Hudson River School. Hill admired and studied the works of these American painters; many of them were his friends. In the 1850s he also copied English master works, which he must have taken from reproductions, since he did not return to England at that time.

In 1859 and 1860 the brothers, Thomas and Edward Hill, were employed at the Gardner, Massachusetts furniture factory for the Levi Heywood Company, which later became the well-known Heywood-Wakefield Company. The brothers "decorated chairs with painted landscapes and baskets of fruit and flowers, plentiful with gold leaf."[28] Thomas decorated for Levi Heywood, president of the company, a magnificent bedroom set, "consisting of bed, bureau, table, commode, and four chairs."[29]

Although, through his industry, Hill seemed always able to make a living, and his paintings were admired publicly and by his fellow artists, he was not satisfied with his progress as a painter. That fact, perhaps combined with the loss of the children, affected his health. Threatened with tuberculosis, Thomas Hill (artist), age thirty-one, decided to move with his family to a milder climate and chose California. His cousin, young Benjamin Hill—who with his wife Jane had followed the Hill family "immigrants" to the Boston area—wrote to his parents in England:

> I received a letter from Uncle Thomas [Thomas Hill–tailor] and they are all well but he has not got anything to do. His son Tom has gone to California because he thinks he can do better there and his health is not very good.[30]

II California 1861–1866

Documentation of the journey to California is limited to the single word "overland," which refers to the route taken by the Thomas Hill (artist) family in 1861, from New England to the far West.[1] If a diary was kept it has not been located. The exact date of arrival in San Francisco is not known, but in 1861 Hill may have worked briefly in the city as a sign and ornamental painter with Charles Hopps and David Kanary.[2]

Hill lost no time, however, in establishing himself as an artist with a studio, which from 1862 through 1864 was located in San Francisco's Mercantile Library Building.[3] In his studio Hill painted portraits and developed oil paintings from sketches taken on tours of the California countryside.

In 1862 he made his first trip to Yosemite Valley, accompanied by William Keith—an engraver who was just beginning to think about landscape painting—and his old friend from Boston days, Virgil Williams.[4] Hill filled his portfolio with sketches which he later used for his great panoramic oil paintings of Yosemite landscapes, works that were to start him on the road to fame and good fortune. His painting, *Byrnes Ferry on the Stanislaus River*, 1862, is one of the fine smaller works resulting from this first visit to Yosemite.

Hill soon returned to the "high Sierra." In July, 1864, he ventured into uncharted wilderness areas in the Kings River Canyon with a prospecting tour, a group which included the mountain man John Bubbs, Tom Carroll, John Beveridge, Henry Kettleson, and others. The terrain became so difficult that some of the party returned to base camp; it is not known if Hill stayed with the party until it became necessary to kill the horses, not only for their own sakes, but also to provide a food supply for the explorers.[5] However, Hill made many sketches and later painted landscapes of the "Bubbs Creek" area.

In 1864, shortly after his return from this adventure, Hill exhibited at the San Francisco Mechanics' Institute Exposition: *Sunset View in Russian River Valley; View of Napa Valley from Soda Springs; View of Lake Tahoe from Western Summit; Emerald Bay; Lake Tahoe;* two *Views of the American River;* six portraits; and one "Fancy Sketch."[6]

Until the completion of the transcontinental railroad in 1869, the San Francisco artists, still so isolated from the rest of the world, formed the nucleus of the congenial, hard-working group, devoted to cooperation among themselves for the general promotion of the arts in California. There were no art galleries, per se, but the art stores provided display areas for the artists' works, which were also exhibited in their studios and at the Mechanics' Institute Industrial Expositions, which did not occur every year.

In 1865 Samuel Brookes, the city's leading painter of still life, organized the California Art Union, patterning its organization after the earlier New York and midwestern art unions, which had provided artists with the opportunity to display and sell their works. Enthusiasm, with accompanying publicity from an admiring press, ran high. Hill was the chosen leader. His painting, *The Trial Scene from the Merchant of Venice*, which he based on the performances in San Francisco by Charles Kean and his wife,[7] was purchased by the Art Union for $700 in gold. Following the 1865 exhibition,[8] Hill received many "puffs"; one critic wrote:

> No. 44, *The Trial Scene*, from the Merchant of Venice, by Thomas Hill...the groupings are fine, the positions anatomically correct, and the draperies well arranged; the colony is natural, and the whole picture shows the skill and judgment of the artist.[9]

Hill also exhibited some of his unsold paintings in the Art Union show: *Portrait: Gentleman; Good Morning; Sugar Loaf Rock; Strawberry Valley; Napa Valley;* and *Near Crystal Springs*.[10]

Benjamin Parke Avery, a professional writer and art critic, who also became a patron of the San Francisco artists, wrote, "Photographic copies of Hill's *Merchant of Venice* had been promised to each subscriber to the California Art Union, but the promise could not be kept when the Art Union, through lack of good management, perhaps, died in its first year."[11]

Avery describes Hill and his works in California before the artist left the state in 1866 to study in Paris:

> Thomas Hill, a young artist of merit, who obtained his tuition in this State, displayed much ability while here from 1862 to 1866, and produced some of the best views of California scenery executed by any painter....There were breadth and boldness in his pictures, with much incident. He introduced figures and animals with capital effect...he executed many large scenic pictures for public houses...but his smaller works are best done and most admired. He also executed some portraits which were finely colored, especially those of women and children.[12]

By 1865 Hill had completed eleven oil panels of Pacific Coast scenery for the banquet room of San Francisco's most famous hostelry of the day, the Lick House.[13] Indeed, by 1865, Hill's opinions and services were sought by many. Frederick Law Olmsted, a California politician whose pet project at the time was to make the Yosemite and the Mariposa Redwood Grove a state park, commissioned Thomas Hill, Virgil Williams, and the pioneer photographer, Carleton E. Watkins, to make a special study of the scenic values of the proposed park and to indicate the way the area might be improved "in the great interests of the public."[14]

Perhaps the 1865 commission was the beginning of the friendship between Hill and photographer Watkins. There is no evidence available that Hill himself took photographs, as did William Keith, to help in the development of his paintings. Nor does photography seem to fit in with Hill's rapid sketch techniques and known methods with the brush in achieving desired light effects. However, no doubt Hill occasionally used photographs—probably taken by others—as there are photographs of landscape subjects

Fig. 5:   EL CAPITAN, 1866
        18 × 26 in.
        Collection of Miss May Dornin.

Fig. 6: WOODS AT FONTAINEBLEAU, 1870
26 × 42 in.
Collection of Kerwin Galleries.

Norton Pearl Photography.

represented in various Hill paintings, which are located in the Holsinger–Cravagan Thomas Hill memorabilia collection of The Oakland Museum's Art Department. Also, in the museum's History Department, there is a collection of photographs taken by Watkins of paintings by Hill. It is likely that Hill recognized Watkins' superior abilities with the camera, and employed his services on occasion, rather than pursuing the art of photography himself.

Hill's industry and accomplishments in California in the 1860s indicate that his health had either improved or was, in fact, restored; again it was time for an important step forward in his career.

III Paris 1866–1867

To broaden his horizons and to improve his contacts and techniques, Thomas Hill (artist), at the age of thirty-seven, left his wife and children in San Francisco and spent most of 1866 and part of 1867 in Europe.[1] He was, by this time, financially able to provide for his family and also to travel, and he made the most of it.

En route, Hill stayed awhile in New York City; his oil painting, *View of the Yo-Semite Valley, California*, was exhibited at the National Academy of Design. The listing in the catalog gives Hill's home address as "California."[2]

In Paris Hill studied six months in the studio of the German painter Paul Friedrich Meyerheim[3] (1842–1915), a specialist in genre and figure painting, who was fourteen

years younger than his pupil. In 1866 Hill was notably skilled in figure and animal painting; he was also accomplished in still–life compositions, and had painted many landscapes. However, it was his sketches of scenes in the forests at Fontainebleau which most attracted Meyerheim, who encouraged the versatile painter to specialize in landscape.[4]

Although Hill sketched in the countryside with the Barbizon painters, it is interesting to note that he did not come under their influence to the extent that George Inness did in the same environment. Hill continued to create his own style, within the confines of Romantic Realism, yet adhering to the individualistic trend which characterized his works for the remainder of his life. It was in Paris that Hill developed distinctive brush strokes, which he learned to adapt for massive effects or for a particular compositional technique. Hill's color selections and blends, in his more mature style, are generally in a low-keyed pink-brown tonality, touched with brighter opaque colors. To obtain contrast, Hill preferred dabs of brighter color, which he applied with a heavy twist of the brush, and subtly worked them into the compositional whole. Rarely did he use the popular technique of the day employing broader planes in balanced *chiaroscuro*.

A quiet man, never "Bohemian" in his style of living, Hill was by nature generous, open-hearted, and even gregarious on occasion in the company of friends.[5] In Paris, Jean-Baptiste Millet admired his work; this opened many doors for the American painter.[6] Thomas Couture

Fig. 7:   BIRTHPLACE OF JOHN GREENLEAF WHITTIER, [1868]
          30 × 46½ in.
          Collection of the Trustees of the Haverhill Public Library.

Fig. 8:   VIEW OF ELEPHANT HEAD FROM
          CRAWFORD HOUSE, 1869
          12⅝ × 18 in.
          Collection of the New Hampshire Historical Society.

Fig. 9: LANDSCAPE WITH OAK TREE, 1869
17½ × 25½ in.
Collection of John H. Garzoli Fine Arts.

also became his advocate. When several of Hill's paintings were displayed at the Paris Universal Exposition of 1867, Couture was enthusiastic with praise.[7] As one newspaper reported, "No pictures by Americans were more favorably received."[8]

In 1867 Hill visited England on his return trip to the United States. It is family legend that he became the sketching companion of Queen Victoria's daughter, Princess Louise, who was also an artist.[9] However, there is no factual documentation available regarding these references to Hill's possible associations with the English court, and there are no known paintings of English scenes by Hill from this period.

When the European tour came to an end in the spring of 1867, Hill was not ready to return to San Francisco. He decided instead to settle in Boston; soon after his arrival there, he sent for his wife and children.[10]

IV New England 1867–1871

In 1867 Thomas Hill (artist) opened a studio in Boston at #49 Studio Building.[1] Virgil Williams was also back in Boston and perhaps it was Williams who persuaded Hill to relocate in New England rather than in California. The artists in the Studio Building held open house receptions every Saturday; Hill soon was the center of attraction. In January, 1868, a critic wrote:

Up one flight we find Mr. Hill's studio. On entering we notice several large pictures of wild and picturesque scenery, and are told by the artist they are views of California.... Virgil Williams has the studio on this floor, in which he has several picturesque compositions of Italian peasants and scenery.[2]

In February, Hill began to paint his grand scale masterpiece of the Yosemite, which he titled *The Yo-Semite Valley*. The landscape is described as oil on canvas, measuring six feet by ten feet, and representing the whole main portion of the spectacular scene.[3]

It staggers Atlantic ideas of altitude and distance. There is in it an energy of inspiration which surpasses the dapper prettiness of our mountain scenery. It is the whole of what Bierstadt gave us half, and a vision of the new world to be open to us by the lengthening arm of the railway to the Pacific.[4]

In March Hill had two new views from California quite equal to his former works.

He is hard at work upon his large picture, and it begins to stand out from the canvas strongly and effectively.... Champney has nearly finished his Conway picture, and he thinks it will be the best view of this beautiful village ever painted.[5]

Hill's *The Yo-Semite Valley*, finished in 1868, was exhibited in June at Childs Gallery in Boston,[6] priced at $10,000[7]. The *Transcript* reported that it represented "quite literally, the sublimest of scenery. It is composed from sketches taken on the spot."[8] The panoramic western landscape painting was selected by Louis Prang of Boston for chromolithographic reproduction. To obtain the best quality results, Prang commissioned Hill to paint a smaller version, and selected William Harring, one of his best staff artists, to transfer the painting to the long series of lithographic stones.[9]

In October, 1868, Hill and his friend, journalist Charles H. Brainard, visited John Greenleaf Whittier's birthplace in East Haverhill, Massachusetts. Hill made a sketch for a painting, while Brainard explored the old house and surrounding woodland. According to Brainard's published account of their day, Hill set up his easel at a vantage point against a stone wall beside a brook. Brainard wrote:

> Returning to the brook-side, where I had left the artist at work, I found him surrounded by a group of men and boys, who looked with intent and evident delight at an admirable sketch in oil colors of the house and barn, and the picturesque scenery.

In conclusion Brainard added:

> Mr. Hill finished a large painting from the beautiful sketch, which has been examined by Mr. Whittier, who pronounces it the most satisfactory picture of his early home.... The picture has been purchased by Prang & Co.... by whom it will shortly be reproduced in chromo-lithography.[10]

By November, Hill's studio was filled with paintings. While he worked on a view of Goodrich Falls, he took orders for larger pictures of White Mountain scenery. At the November Studio Building reception, Hill displayed sketches of Niagara Falls and the White Mountains.[11]

Hill may have been ill in 1869, or he may have made a brief visit to California. Although still listed with a studio in Boston and with a residence in Cambridge, there is little evidence that he was there. In San Francisco his paintings *On the Yuba River* and *Table Mountain* were displayed at Snow & Roos Art Gallery.[12]

1870, however, was a major year for Hill in Boston. His great painting, *The White Mountain Notch, New Hampshire*, attracted large crowds at Childs & Company, where Prang lithographs were hung side by side with the paintings on which they were based.[13]

In October, when the foliage was still brilliant Hill was commissioned by a Boston family to paint the famous old Boston hostelry, *The Wayside Inn*. The painting and Longfellow's poem, *Tales of a Wayside Inn*, came out about the same time. Describing Hill's painting, a critic wrote, "In his delineation of the graceful branching elm trees, Hill is said to excel even his famous contemporary painter of out-of-door scenes, George Ines" [*sic*].[14] The painting was exhibited in New York, then chromolithographed by Prang & Company. Louis Prang purchased the painting for his personal collection.[15]

Meanwhile, Hill was not forgotten by the San Francisco resident artists and press. While his friends were

Fig. 10: GREAT CANYON OF THE SIERRAS—YOSEMITE, 1871
72 × 120 in.
Collection of the Crocker Art Museum.

Fig. 11: *preceding pages*
YOSEMITE VALLEY (FROM BELOW SENTINEL DOME, AS SEEN FROM ARTIST'S POINT), 1876
72 × 120 in.
Collection of The Oakland Museum
Gift of the Kahn Foundation.

delighted with reports of his success, the *Alta California*, perhaps piqued at the failure of their former favorite to return from Europe directly to San Francisco, remarked:

> ...We hear occasionally from our artists abroad. William Keith is in Germany.[16] Thomas Hill has taken up his abode in Boston. We notice a marked change in his manner. He has ignored that free sketchy style in which he was so felicitous, and adopted the dry impasto mode of the French school. In the latter he is a probationer; but time may ripen him into a master.[17]

San Francisco, however, had not long to wait for the return of its erstwhile adopted son and leader of California artists. Sometime between February 10 and March 21, 1871 the artist and his family voyaged via the Isthmus of Panama to San Francisco, intending to stay.[18] The artist's health had failed again; once more he sought a milder climate, and chose the place where he was already established.

V California and the Art Boom of the 1870s

Thomas Hill could not have returned to California at a better time. San Francisco as a major Pacific coast port boomed in the 1870s. The city, no longer isolated, and rich with the returns from railroad and Comstock silver wealth, had developed a stable population of approximately 200,000 people. The rich, including those who became patrons of the arts—the Stanfords, the Crockers, the Fairs, and others—were furnishing their unique and elaborate mansions. California's picturesque themes were still in demand, and with commissioned works varying in subject matter depending on the whims of *nouveau riche* patronage, the art of painting flourished wildly.

Although the boom days came to an end in 1879, in the interim, the best-known painters became wealthy themselves. Among these, Thomas Hill and William Keith—who in the five years of Hill's absence had made great progress as an artist—became California's leading landscape painters.

Perhaps by chance, Hill's arrival in 1871 coincided with the organization of the San Francisco Art Association, which was formally set in motion on March 28, with Juan B. Wandesforde as president, Frederick Whymper as Secretary, and a membership including Hill.[1] The new organization moved swiftly. In May the first formal reception was held at the San Francisco Mercantile Library with a handsome display of paintings on easels.[2]

Hill was soon busy in his Tucker Building studio filling local orders for portraits and landscapes. However, he did not neglect his former eastern connections. In 1871 and 1872 his paintings were displayed at the Boston Athenaeum.[3] His *Great Canyon of the Sierras*, 1871—another grand scale Yosemite masterpiece painted in Boston from sketches taken in California in the 1860s—

was exhibited in New York City. Quoting Hill, "I was awarded the [bronze] medal at the Palette Club for that picture."[4]

In 1872 Hill sold *Great Canyon of the Sierras*, 1871, and his famed *Yo-Semite Valley*, 1868, in California. Railroad magnate Charles Crocker of San Francisco purchased *Yo-Semite Valley*, 1868, for $10,000.[5] His brother, Judge E.B. Crocker of Sacramento, acquired *Great Canyon of the Sierras*, 1871, which is still in the collection of the Crocker Art Museum. Although sources vary, the price paid was either $5,000 or $10,000.[6]

Also in 1872 Hill exhibited *Niagara Falls; Moonlight;* and *Point Lobos* at the spring show of the San Francisco Art Association, which was staged in more spacious new quarters on Pine Street.[7]

Hill spent the summer months with Virgil Williams at the latter's summer cabin in California's Sonoma Valley under the shadow of Mount St. Helena. This became one of Hill's favorite retreats; he painted the cabin in its landscape setting, along with many other landscapes and scenes of the area.

In the fall, Hill and Williams returned to San Francisco, where the social life, enjoyed harmoniously by an intermingling of the artists and their patrons, picked up in expectation of the new season.

In 1873 Hill became a member of the Bohemian Club, beginning a lifetime affiliation.[8] Again he was active in Boston, with paintings exhibited at the Boston Art Club,[9] the Boston Athenaeum,[10] and in a private competition sale at a gallery in Boston.[11] In June his painting *The Royal Arches of the Yosemite*, displayed at the San Francisco Art Association, drew unfavorable criticism.[12] Other paintings by Hill in this show are listed as *Russian River Valley; Forest Scene; Home of the Eagle; Scene in the Bois de Boulogne; Shepherd Boy; Connecticut River; After Troyon;* and *Venice*. All the paintings were owned by the artist and only *Home of the Eagle* was marked "for sale."[13]

Hill, age forty-three, was no longer described as "one of our talented young artists."

> Although the community has lost Bierstadt, it retains Thomas Hill, who is building a commodious studio, and has no present intention of deserting the Coast. Our young artists...have little wherewith to compare their works,...hence we rejoice when artists of eminence come among us, more especially when, like both the above-named gentlemen, they are ready to advise and encourage struggling talent.[14]

On December 10, 1873, the Art Association staged a reception celebrating the coming opening of the California School of Design

> ...with a display of casts and models from which the students are to learn the limning of the human form divine.... This morning, were assembled many of the artists whose works hang on the walls. Tom Hill anxiously surveyed the scene and wondered whether he could make room for another picture.[15]

Hill's large painting, *The Headwaters of the Saco*, and Bierstadt's *San Joaquin River* were centers of attraction, receiving press mention.[16]

The Art School, the first of its kind in the West, opened on February 9, 1874, at the Association's third location, still larger accommodations at 313 Pine Street.[17] Virgil Williams was hired as the school's first director and teacher. In that year the Association's officers were: San Francisco's mayor, William Alvord, president; Thomas Hill and printer Edward Bosqui, vice presidents; and author B.P. Avery, Secretary.[18] Hill also was appointed in 1874 one of several trustees for the Bohemian Club.[19]

Hill was indefatigable; his prolific accomplishments are measured in the long lists of his works shown in California exhibitions in the 1870s and 1880s. Increasingly, the subjects became Yosemite landscapes, and Hill spent more and more time in "the Valley." Perhaps that is one reason why he was reluctant to take pupils; his time for his own work was too precious. Even his sons, Edward Rufus Hill and Thomas Virgil Troyon Hill, who both became artists through their own inclinations, received minimal instruction from their father.

> Mr. Hill's eldest son, Edward R. Hill, was an artist of very creditable paintings, his style was not unlike his father's but more after Mr. William Keith's paintings, with warm colors of reds, browns and yellow...
> another son [Thomas V. T. Hill] painted fairly well without any instructions...and attempted to copy his father's style of painting and also his signature, but was not a success at it.[20]

In the fall of 1874 Hill exhibited nine paintings at the Mechanics' Institute Fair.[21] One title listed as *Mount Hood* indicates that Hill by this time had traveled far north; titles of other paintings of this period further disclose that his journeys may have taken him as far as British Columbia.

In November, 1874, Hill participated in a joint sale by the artists of San Francisco at Newhall's art gallery.

> Thomas Hill, in addition to a number of characteristic landscapes, has a still life study of a hare, a gun and some quail, rendered in his best style. The roses in the background are not up to his customary mark.[22]

This sale was followed by the seventh reception of the Art Association, which featured 112 paintings and "too large a crowd for comfort....Thomas Hill contributes two paintings, representing the *Falls of Staubbach*, in Switzerland, and *Lake Geneva*. The frames are oval topped... something of a novelty in California."[23] Hill also exhibited at the show still another grand scale Yosemite landscape, *The Heart of the Sierras*, which was purchased by E.J. "Lucky" Baldwin, a patron of California art who owned a large ranch in southern California.[24]

Joseph Roos, formerly a partner in the Snow & Roos art store, had opened his own art establishment in 1874 at 20 Post Street, which included art supplies and the Beaux-Arts Gallery, a small but "tastefully fitted up" display area where Hill and other artists exhibited their paintings.[25] In 1875 Hill joined Roos in a partnership; in June he traveled to the East where he purchased eastern paintings for the

Fig. 12: *opposite page*
PALO ALTO SPRING, 1878
86⅞ × 138¼ in.
Collection of the Stanford University Museum of Art
Stanford Family Collection.

Fig. 13: PAPER MILL CREEK, MARIN COUNTY
14 × 20¼ in.
Collection of The Fine Arts Museums of San Francisco.

gallery.[26] On July 31 the *News Letter* noted his return, with a quote: "[Hill] came back to us from the East rejuvenated—or as he says 'Feeling like a bird—so phoenixed.' "[27]

Meanwhile, Hill's paintings were bringing higher prices; two paintings, "small in size," sold at the Beaux-Arts Gallery for a total of $2,000.[28] According to various family sources and published reports, Hill was averaging $20,000 per year, which at the time represented a sizable income for an American artist, especially for an artist working and living in California.

In January, 1876, excitement ran high in San Francisco art circles as some resident artists prepared for the coming Centennial Exposition in Philadelphia. Thomas Hill received numerous press mentions; one critic expressed the fear that if Hill exhibited a picture in Philadelphia before it could be displayed in his home city, "it would be bought and never returned."[29]

On January 15 the same source wondered if it was "ethical" for Hill to ask $5,000 for his just-completed painting, *Donner Lake*, "which duplicates [*Great*] *Canyon of the Sierras*."[30] Whatever the case *Donner Lake* and a large Yosemite landscape were shipped for exhibition at the Centennial show which opened on May 10. Hill was awarded a bronze medal and a diploma for "best in landscape."[31]

In April, 1876, still another large Hill Yosemite landscape was purchased for San Francisco's newly finished Palace Hotel. The painting was displayed in the grand parlor, flanked on each side by "scenes of the Sierras by the same talented artist"—and a fourth Hill painting was placed over the piano.[32]

In May, 1876, Hill bought out Joseph Roos & Co., renamed the business "Thos. Hill & Co.," and kept the Beaux-Arts Gallery.[33] The business became a family affair, providing a sales outlet not only for Thomas Hill and other artists, but also for "Edward Hill." It is not known if "Edward" in this case was Thomas' son, Edward Rufus Hill, or his brother, the New England landscape painter Edward Hill, who visited San Francisco on occasion. Thomas also brought into the business his brother William Francis Hill, who had meanwhile earned an enviable reputation in Boston as a cabinetmaker.[34]

Hill traveled East again and visited the Centennial Exposition. While away, he sent what may have been a series relating to one theme to the 1876 Mechanics' Industrial Fair:

> Among the works of local artists, landscapes were, as usual, placed on the first rank. Thomas Hill sent us his paintings of *The Great Master*. W. Keith and E. Deakin also sent us works to be noted for their merit; J. Tavernier, whose compositions are so peculiar and attractive, would have required a critic of the first order to analyze them. Norton Bush, W.L. Marple; R.D. Yelland, etc. etc. were also well represented.[35]

A description of Thomas Hill in 1877 is conveniently available and, judging from all other accounts, probably accurate:

Thomas Hill would never be suspected of being an artist. His style of dress resembles that of a well-to-do rural resident more than that of a city denizen, and his general carriage and pose is not at all suggested of the aesthetic. In conversation, however, he makes himself felt and betrays intelligence and considerable culture. Mr. Hill is a man of large capabilities and much power, and probably there is no painter in the country, who paints more rapidly. It is related of him that on one occasion he painted six 18 × 24 pictures in nine hours.[36]

In April, what was advertised as Hill's "entire collection of paintings" was auctioned in the rooms of the Art Association.[37] Apparently, however, the auction was not a success, or perhaps Hill kept his best canvases out of the sale. In June the *Chronicle* noted that Hill was spending several weeks in St. Helena, and provided additional information that his well-known painting, *Purissima Creek*— first displayed in January—and paintings of *His Son and his Dog Prince; Stockton Ranch;* and *Mount St. Helena* had recently been seen in the artist's studio.[38]

Reference to Thomas Hill and his son Edward sketching on the line of the California-based Central Pacific railroad in July, 1877,[39] may relate to Hill's most controversial painting, *The Driving of the Last Spike*, 1881.

For some time Leland Stanford, president of the Central Pacific Railroad, who had served as California's governor in 1862 and 1863, had been discussing with Hill the subject for a grand scale, major work, a depiction of the ceremony held on May 10, 1869, at Promontory Point, Utah, when the Central Pacific tracks and the Union Pacific tracks met and were joined, creating, at last, a transcontinental railroad.

Hill began the painting in 1877, believing, no doubt, that Stanford, who had been a generous patron in the past, would of course pay for it. He was also busy with other work. In the fall of 1877 he completed large oil panels depicting Yosemite and other California themes for the redecoration of the Lick House Hotel.[40]

Hill participated in the Mechanics' Institute Fair in 1877 and was rewarded with two bronze medals.[41] Paintings exhibited were *Mount Shasta*, owned by the artist, and seven other works owned by Captain J.M. McDonald: *High Sierras; Winter in New Hampshire; Castle Lake; Fruit Piece; Dawson's Ranch; Wreck of the Pilot Boat Cousins;* and *Sketching*.[42]

In 1878 the great boom of the 1870s was not quite over. The art school was flourishing; local patrons were still buying. Thomas Hill, now age forty-nine, was a wealthy man, as well as an example often touted. In 1879, Theophilus d'Estrella, a deaf-mute pupil at the School of Design, was advised in note form by his teacher, Virgil Williams:

It [a sketch of mine] is awfully careless. Do not try after Hill. Try...any great French masters. Tom Hill has a great deal of knowledge and can afford to neglect details, and there is always so much evidence of knowledge in his work that the most careless

Fig. 14: THE DRIVING OF THE LAST SPIKE
8 ft. ⅜ in. × 12 ft. ½ in.
State of California, Department of Parks and Recreation, California State Railroad Museum.

26

Fig. 15: CALIFORNIA QUAIL, 1881
13⅞ × 20¾ in.
Collection of The Oakland Museum
Gift of the Kahn Foundation.

Fig. 16: *opposite page*
CALIFORNIA, 1879
42 × 70¼ in.
Private collection.

sketch of his passes for good. You have his careless-ness without his knowledge.[43]

VI California 1879–1884

Hill sold his Post Street gallery in 1879 to Snow & Company; he is listed in that year as a landscape and marine painter with a studio at 1227 Turk Street.[1]

In March the family moved from San Francisco across the bay to Oakland. On March 5, the artist's wife Charlotte M. Hill, "in consideration of the sum of Fifteen thousand Dollars Gold Coin," purchased a twenty room house on a ten acre estate on Seminary Avenue in Oakland.[2] Photo-graphs show a long drive leading from an ornamental iron gate past fountains. In this pleasant domicile, Hill, with his wife and their nine children, had a country estate for their settled enjoyment.

However, these pleasures were short-lived. In 1879—the year of the move—an economic depression struck Cali-fornia. At the same time, local art patronage came literally to a standstill. The rich still had money to spend, but they had tired of "California" art. Instead, they traveled in Europe collecting old master works; in some cases they acquired "modern" works of a more impressionistic nature.

According to all accounts, Hill, who had been selling his major landscapes in a price range of four and five figures, was not a shrewd investor. It is also evident that he had spent lavishly in the halcyon years and was unprepared for the sudden and dramatic decline in the local demand for paintings by California artists. Also, for two years, he had allocated a great deal of time to what he called the "Spike picture" at the expense of other opportunities.

Hill did, however, continue to exhibit. In 1879 he won the gold medal for "Best Exhibition in Art" at the California State Fair in Sacramento.[3] At the 1880 spring show at the Art Association his paintings with prices are listed as: *The Short Way Home* at $1,000; *Cattle (Even-ing)* at $500; *Salmon Festival of Northern Indians* at $1,500; and *Deer (Early Morning)* at $500.[4] *The Salmon Festival* was highly praised. "If there was nothing else to look upon," wrote a critic, "that exquisite bit of coloring would be well worth the price of admission."[5]

But Hill's paintings did not sell. In May, 1880 it was reported:

Thomas Hill has not sold a picture for eight months past, and a similar need of patronage has been the lot of the entire artists' colony....some are taking pupils ...Hill, however, goes to England, taking *The Last Spike* with him.[6]

Hill did not go to England. Instead he spent the summer with his brother, landscape painter Edward Hill of Boston, sketching and painting in the White Mountains.[7] In October the *Chronicle* reported that Hill would return to California for his family and locate them in New York City "where he plans to remain at least two years."[8]

In November Hill returned to his Oakland home.[9] As

he added the last touches to the "Spike picture," intentions to leave were set aside until the unveiling and disposal of the painting could take place. The painting was first exhibited privately at the Art Association in January, 1881, "to a number of Hill's friends, after nearly four years of arduous labor."[10] In February there was a formal unveiling in the State Capitol, Sacramento, "at Governor Perkins' reception in the State Assembly Chamber."[11]

The Driving of the Last Spike, 1881, is probably the most important railroad depiction on canvas, although—after Leland Stanford had persuaded the artist to make numerous changes regarding individuals represented—perhaps not aesthetically or historically so. The huge painting originally measured eight by twelve feet. It presents in Hill's own words, "about 400 figures, seventy of which are portraits." The eye of the viewer focuses on the central figure depicting Stanford—who in 1869 was President of the Central Pacific Railroad—poised with hammer raised to pound in the last spike joining the two converging railroad tracks.[12]

Hill now faced the great tragedy of his career. After Charles Crocker objected to the prominence given to Stanford in the painting, the latter not only rejected the work, he also disclaimed that any commission or agreement had been made by him with the artist. This was the beginning of a long and bitter struggle on Hill's part to properly dispose of the painting.[13]

According to Hill's daughter, Adeline, she was present when Stanford refused to take the picture. The grim occasion took place in Hill's San Francisco studio in the Flood Building. She said:

> In this room I saw and heard Stanford refuse to take it. Saw grandfather [father] lay the picture on the floor and hoist it up *face* to the wall. I heard him say to Stanford as he opened the door, "Goodby, Mr. Stanford." *Spike* had a redwood frame grandfather [father] made himself.[14]

Hill remained in California and is listed as "Artist" at the Seminary Avenue address in the 1880–1881 Oakland City Directory. A boost to his morale soon came with the 1881 spring show at the Art Association. While the *Alta California* reported, "The place of honor in the center of the north wall is given to a picture by Thomas Hill—*A Birch Forest in Autumn*,"[15] the *Chronicle*, after praising the same painting, also mentioned his display of sketches:

> ...Mr. Hill has spread a perfect feast of such pleasures for every lover of Nature by the display of his sketches. They are simply bewildering in their variety of scene and feeling...we gaze and wonder at the artist's industry and patience and admire his genius.[16]

Again Hill spent the summer painting in New Hampshire. Thomas, his brother, Edward, and H.A. Fergeron of New York City headquartered together at the Profile Hotel,[17] located at the foot of "The Old Man of the Mountains," in the White Mountains.[18]

Returning to California in the late summer, Hill exhibited three paintings at the State Fair. He received eight points for one painting and an award of sixteen dollars.[19] He also participated in the Mechanics' Institute Fair with his *Yosemite Valley, Early Morning*, which was described as a view of El Capitan "filled with a verve and brio...the picture is fully-worthy of a man whose reputation is American, although California can claim him as a local artist."[20]

Sales, however, continued to be minimal. On March 9, 1882, Hill staged a public auction sale at the Art Association. During the sale, Hill stood beside the auctioneers, Joseph Eldridge and George Ludington, who assured the buyers that the prices offered were "Murder! yes murder with malice, for the pictures would be worth a fortune if the artist should die...and Tom may die; yes, he may die."[21]

Although all but four of the paintings were sold, the prices per painting ranged in the low hundreds; the major works, *Mount Shasta from Castle Lake; Rescue of the Innocents; The Salmon Festival;* and *Franconia Notch*, were withdrawn due to low bids. All the sketches sold at prices ranging from thirty-five to seventy-five dollars.[22]

Hill, accompanied by one of his daughters, spent the summer in Yosemite.[23] After their return to Oakland, Hill entered ten paintings in the Mechanics' Institute Fair display. An eleventh painting, *Mount Shasta*, is listed in the catalog as owned by Hill's artist friend, Henry Raschen.[24]

In the spring of 1883 Hill's health declined again. To recuperate, he spent several months in Yosemite where he built a studio on the Valley floor in the lower village area near the home of famed Galen Clark, known as "Guardian of the Valley."[25] The lengthy "vacation" proved worthwhile. In July Hill's "recent illness...and recovery" was noted by the press.[26]

In regard to his art, Hill could not have been entirely idle, however. In the fall of 1883 he exhibited a fresh display of Yosemite landscapes, in addition to eight other paintings depicting miscellaneous subjects, at the Mechanics' Fair. His reward was a ten dollar premium for "Meritorious Works in Oils and Water Colors."[27]

In December Hill participated in the first annual auction sale staged by members of the Art Association. But the sale was not a success. In spite of a large crowd and spirited bidding "only a few pictures were knocked down at sums approaching their real value. Among them were ...Hill's *Trout Stream*, $45...the elegant *Brook Scene with Cattle*, by Hill, was sold to Thomas Jennings for $290."[28]

In 1884 Hill was awarded the coveted Temple Silver Medal for his landscape, *Yosemite Valley, General View from Bridal Veil Meadow*, which was included in the annual exhibition at the Pennsylvania Academy of the Fine Arts.[29] He displayed the same painting at the spring exhibition of the San Francisco Art Association. A critic wrote:

> ...Leading lights are missing, notably Tavernier, Yelland and Bradford...Thomas Hill keeps to his early love and has a large picture of the Yosemite Valley from Bridal Veil Meadow...it seems to excel any others of this subject we have seen.[30]

Fig. 17: AMONG THE GIANT REDWOODS, YOSEMITE, 1884
46½ × 28 in.
Collection of Kennedy Galleries, Inc.

Fig. 18: GIANT GEYSER, *ca.* 1880
20½ × 14 in.
Collection of Arthur J. Phelan, Jr.

VII The Yosemite Years 1884–1908

During this period a rift occurred between Thomas Hill and his wife. The reasons have always been a closely guarded family secret abounding in unsubstantiated rumors. Charlotte Hill continued to live at the Seminary Avenue address in Oakland while her husband's activities led him far afield. In the summer of 1884 the artist returned to Yosemite where he found that a great windstorm had demolished his studio on the Valley floor. Hill and his son Edward, who had accompanied him, stayed at the Wawona Hotel located twenty-five miles south of Yosemite and six miles from the Mariposa Grove of giant Sequoia redwoods.[1]

In August Hill decided to travel to new places. His landscapes of the Yellowstone Park area—a series of paintings in which the artist adapted his use of color to the magnificent and different terrain—resulted from several weeks he spent sketching in that unique wilderness.[2]

Hill wintered (1884–1885) in New Orleans where he exhibited *The Last Spike* at the World's Fair. Strange rumors of his activities drifted across the continent to San Francisco art circles. The artist's son, Robert Hill, was interviewed by the press:

> Robert Hill is smiling at the wild reports about his father. He says that there is not a shadow of truth in the report that his respected parent has purchased a plantation on the Mississippi. He also denies that Hill, senior, has started a tannery for dressing alligator hides...in fact Mr. Hill is not in the South at present. The last letter received from him bore a Boston postmark.[3]

Hill did visit New England where he still maintained his membership in the Boston Art Club. When he returned to California in the spring of 1885, he left paintings behind in Boston, which were displayed in May at Noyes & Blakeslee Gallery.[4]

The artist returned to California in time for the April, 1885 wedding of his fourth daughter, Estella Louise, to John Stephen Washburn, a Yosemite Valley commissioner and one of the proprietors of the Wawona Hotel. The fact that both parents of the bride were present indicates that a temporary truce between the artist and his wife had taken place for the sake of the event. Following the elaborate ceremony at the Hill family estate in Seminary Park, Oakland, "the newly wedded pair, accompanied by Mr. Thomas Hill, Mrs. Edward Hill, and other members of the family, started for Monterey, where they will remain for a few days and then go to Yosemite."[5]

The wedding marked the passing of an era of elegance for Thomas Hill and his wife. Within a few months it became necessary to sell the Seminary Avenue estate, which was heavily mortgaged; the sum realized was only "Six Thousand five hundred Dollars Gold."[6]

In 1885 there is no available listing for Thomas Hill or the family. In 1886 the artist is listed in the San Francisco directory with a studio at 411½ California Street and a residence at 1707 Polk Street. He is also listed in 1886 as a resident at Big Tree Station (Wawona) in the Great Register of Mariposa County, which adds his physical description: "Five feet eight inches height; light complexion; grey eyes and brown hair."

In March, 1887, Charlotte Hill acquired a homestead residence valued at $4,000 at the corner of Piedmont and Webster Streets, Oakland.[7] Although this address, with subsequent street number changes, is listed under the artist's name in most years from 1887 until 1903, he probably lived there seldom, if at all.

Hill lived most of the time in the Yosemite area, although he also kept a studio in San Francisco. Unless on sketching tours or business trips, Hill spent his summers at the Wawona Hotel and his winters in nearby Raymond, a small town with a railroad connection. His daughter and her husband were a great help to him. The artist lived at the Wawona Hotel in rooms 10 and 11; in 1886 the Washburns had built for him a three-room studio next door. Hill filled the studio with picturesque items; however, only his paintings were for sale.

> After dinner [at the Wawona Hotel] it was the prac-
> tice for the Washburns to skillfully direct guests over
> to Mr. Hill's studio, where specimens of mounted
> animals as well as a fine collection of war imple-
> ments, very likely attracted as much attention as
> his paintings.[8]

However, Hill had not retired. On frequent trips to San Francisco he stayed at the Palace Hotel; sometimes the Washburns came with him. He also continued to participate in California exhibitions. Describing the 1886 spring exhibition at the San Francisco Art Association a critic wrote:

> Entering the large salon, attention is first demanded
> by the works of Thomas Hill....The picture...
> treating of the valley, is full of his happy effects of
> atmosphere and falling mist...in a word the picture
> is simply "Hill's Yosemite."...Two other canvases of
> his treat of the Yellowstone region...with no little
> degree of strength....The least said of *A Tourist
> in Yosemite* the better...in it the artist is not at
> his best.[9]

On May 17, 1886, the artist's father, Thomas Hill (tailor) died at the age of eighty-two at his home in Gardner, Massachusetts.[10] His son Thomas Hill (artist) traveled to New England. The date of his arrival is not clear; however, he stayed to see the fall colors. Again, Hill painted with Benjamin Champney in the White Mountains.[11]

Hill's friend Virgil Williams, the beloved Director of the California School of Design, died unexpectedly on December 18, 1886. Two days later the Art Association's Board of Directors met to appoint his replacement:

> Mr. Thomas Hill being present...by invitation,
> volunteered his services to take charge for a time
> without pay. Mr. Bosqui then offered the following.
> Resolved that the committee of the School of Design
> accept the generous offer of Mr. T. Hill to assume
> charge and direction of the school without com-
> pensation.[12]

Fig. 19: YELLOWSTONE FALLS
18½ × 24½ in.
Collection of Mr. and Mrs. Charles C. Smith.

Fig. 20: FISHING PARTY IN THE MOUNTAINS
24 × 20 in.
Collection of The Fine Arts Museums of San Francisco.

Almost simultaneously, on December 22, an advertisement was published offering: "Thomas Hill's Great Sale of Oil Paintings at Auction This Day...Art Gallery of...the Art Association...and Sketches, etc....Easton & Eldridge Auctioneers."[13]

Published results of this sale—which included scenes in the White Mountains, Oregon, Washington Territory, Yellowstone Park, and California including Yosemite and the Big Trees[14]—have not been located, but no doubt Hill was depending heavily on the sale when he accepted—probably through blind emotion—the post at the school "without compensation."

For the second time in his life Thomas Hill "ran away" when faced with an unsuitable burden. In his youth, when forced to contribute his earnings to family support, he had left home without notice to work for himself in Boston. In 1887 the directorship of the School of Design became an impossible task. The answer came when the famed naturalist, John Muir, commissioned Hill to paint the great Muir Glacier located at Glacier Bay, Alaska. Muir usually preferred the landscapes of his close friend, William Keith; however, in this case he chose Hill "because he could paint ice better than Keith."[15]

Apparently Hill did not inform the school of his intentions, or perhaps he gave short notice. In any case, the school was left high and dry when Hill, accompanied by his son, Edward, voyaged by steamer to Glacier Bay.[16]

The commissioned painting, *Muir Glacier*, is in the collection of The Oakland Museum, the gift of John Muir's descendants. The painting is undated but was probably done in the winter of 1887–1888. On March 4, 1888, Hill wrote a quaint letter to Muir acknowledging payment of $500 "to settle for the Painting of Muir Glacier."[17] A similar painting owned by the Anchorage Historical and Fine Arts Museum bears the date 1889. A variety of Alaskan and Canadian scenes by Hill resulted from this journey.

In fact, of the nineteen paintings by Hill which were reproduced in *Picturesque California*, published in 1888, two are depictions of the Muir Glacier area. This publication, which relates to the entire Pacific Coast of North America, and features text and "photo-gravure" illustrations reproduced from paintings by a number of artists, was edited by Muir.[18]

In the Heart of the Sierras, a 496-page book featuring text and 154 illustrations by California artists and photographers, was compiled and published by James Mason Hutchings of San Francisco and Yosemite in 1888.

In his preface Hutchings wrote: "The designs for the embossed covers, in black and gold, are by Mr. Thomas Hill, the eminent and well-known California artist, who has generously furnished other sketches for this work."

The frontispiece is a reproduction of a painting by C.D. Robinson entitled *In the Heart of the Sierras*. It depicts Yosemite Valley with Half Dome in the background and a grizzly bear standing in profile on a jutting ledge, dominating the right center foreground.

The book contains descriptions of Hill's and Robinson's studios and includes tactful comparisons of their styles.[19]

In the fall of 1888 Hill won a premium award of $30 at the Mechanics' Fair for exhibiting *Mount Tacoma [Mount Rainier] W.T.; Royal Arches and Dome, Yosemite;* and *Bass Fishing (Lake George).*[20]

The year 1889 was quite uneventful for Hill. Again he spent most of his time at Wawona, and again he exhibited in San Francisco and at the State Fair. He was still seeking a suitable home for the "Spike picture." On November 22, on Palace Hotel stationery, he wrote to Leland Stanford:

> My Dear Sir:
>
> I take the liberty of approaching you again in regard to my Painting of the Last Spike, as you are the only person I can look to for any assistance in the matter.
>
> Fearing the destruction of the work by being "rolled and hidden in the dark for so long" I offered the picture to the State last winter, the result of my action proved how weak I was.
>
> It has been suggested by many friends of yours who are kindly disposed to the Artist that the picture should find a home in the new University your generosity has founded, and like your generous gift commemorate one of the greatest events in the History of the State.
>
> As I have outlived my expectations, it is no longer a question of dollars and cents, but the preservation of my greatest achievement.
>
> Trusting I may not be compelled to offer it at Public Sale, I await your answer to my last appeal with great anxiety.
>
> Very respectfully your obdt. servant
> Thomas Hill[21]

In the early 1890s Hill continued his life style in the same pattern. At Wawona his studio became a point of great interest to tourists. Hill sold many paintings, including depictions of landscapes and giant redwoods hastily oil-sketched on redwood panels and shingles.

He also continued with activities in San Francisco and Sacramento. In 1890 at the Art Association spring show he served as a supplementary juror with R.D. Yelland, A. Weinert, and sculptor F. Marion Wells. However, the only painting by Hill in the show was a Yosemite landscape owned by George H. Redding.[22]

In September at the State Fair Hill was awarded a gold medal for a painting of Muir Glacier.[23]

The year 1891 was much the same. Shirley Sargent in her book *Yosemite's Historic Wawona* gives glimpses of Hill's pleasant life at Wawona in this period. Hill had the opportunity to enjoy the companionship of his grandchild, Clarence Washburn.[24] In San Francisco in May the artist exhibited *The Grand Canyon of the Colorado* and *Sir Donald Peak in the Selkirk Mountains, Canadian Pacific* at the Art Association show. Both paintings were marked "For Sale."[25] Hill undoubtedly met with the American landscape painter George Inness who was the guest of William Keith in San Francisco; Inness, who had probably

painted with Hill from time to time in New Hampshire, also participated in the show.[26] Later, Hill told his son, Thomas V. T. Hill, "Innes [*sic*] says that Raw Sienna is 'God Almighty' and his pictures sang with it...he uses nothing else." Then he added, "He uses ocre and black with great effect."[27]

A review of the State Fair art show in October reveals that although most California artists were still suffering from economic stagnation some improvement was noted:

> Norton Bush is back from Sacramento. He reports with pride that more pictures were sold at the State Fair this year than ever before, the number being ten. The fair often closes without the sale of a single picture....Among the medal winners were Oscar Kunath, Hugo Fisher, Chris Jorgensen, Mrs. Alice H. Chittenden, R.D. Yelland, Thomas Hill, Lee Lash, William Keith, Eva Withrow, E. Narjot and M. Strauss.[28]

In 1892 Hill broke his routine with a trip to the East and to New England. Again he enjoyed one of his greatest pleasures—painting in the White Mountains. On this occasion Hill and his brother Edward headquartered at Glen House, Pinkham Notch, New Hampshire, with a program of extended walking tours.[29]

In December Hill prepared for the World's Columbian Exposition scheduled to take place from May 1 to October 30, 1893. "He plans to send to Chicago *The Last Spike*," wrote a critic. "Plus twelve paintings of Yosemite...Hill made the frames. These Yosemite paintings are now snowbound in Yosemite and cannot be sketched for the paper."[30]

In January, 1893, Hill was reportedly ill and not painting; in fact, he was advised by his physician not to work.[31] Hill, now age sixty-four, probably overtaxed his strength preparing for the great show. According to his daughter Adeline, her father was a late riser but a tireless worker: "He worked most any time....Very temperamental and given to tantrums...worked in an old coat, never in a smock...more disorderly than most artists—careless with tubes, etc."[32]

When the great fair opened in May the Art Gallery of the California Building displayed at least sixty-one works by California artists. Hill's listing includes his address as "Wawona, Cal." His contributions, all landscapes, oil on canvas or oil on panel, are listed as:

> *California.* A scene near Los Gatos. (Loaned by Mrs. Wm. Lyle, San Francisco).
> *Driving the Last Spike of the Central and Union Pacific Railroads, with Portraits of all Prominent Persons present at the time* (West Gallery).
> *Muir Glacier, Alaska.*
> [Triptych]: *The Grizzly Giant.* Largest tree in the world. (Panel). *Wawona.* Gateway to Yosemite Valley and Mariposa Grove of Big Trees. (Central picture).
> *Big Tree, Wawona.* (Panel).
> *Yosemite Valley from Inspiration Point.*[33]

Hill traveled by train to the Exposition. "Another day has passed," he wrote in an undated diary entry.[34]

Fig. 21: MUIR GLACIER, ALASKA
36 × 54¼ in.
Collection of The Oakland Museum
Gift of Mr. and Mrs. Richard R. Hanna.

Fig. 22: HUNTER WITH RABBIT AND DOG
14 × 21 in.
Collection of Walter A. Nelson-Rees and James L. Coran.

Apparently, time was still precious to him. The artist jotted informal notes in his Bank of California passbook which describe in detail his journey, both ways, and the fair itself. Hill's references to the art galleries "where miles of paintings are displayed" are unique:

> Of all the nations represented I like the German paintings best—the Germans are conscientious workers that try to paint nature as we see it. Other schools like the French, merely give you a suggestion, an impression of the Thing which the observer must complete according to his own taste. This they call poetic Art. I call it *Rott* [sic].[35]

Although Hill's disdain of impressionistic art and other trends leading to "modernism" is so clearly stated, for all the realism of his landscapes, his scenes are freely painted. With sweeping brush strokes Hill created the image of the western American landscape. In expressing his concept of the Pacific coast wilderness, Hill became perhaps the most interpretive painter of his time. Even his notes to his son reveal that Hill was closer to "modernism" than he himself could believe. He advised son Thomas:

> Don't paint paws on your figures, a dab of color is enough. . . . Accidental effects can only be gotten with a big brush, I depend entirely on accident—you have no idea how much is produced that way. . . . It is not necessary to work the cattle up they are only for effect—dabs of color [will do].[36]

Returning from the Chicago Fair to the West Coast,

Hill took a northerly route to Tacoma, Washington. Again he sketched the scenic Cascade peaks in Washington and Oregon before returning to the San Francisco Bay Area and to Wawona.[37]

In the fall, Hill was praised as a great colorist when a large Hill *Yosemite*—in fact, the painting exhibited in the Chicago Fair art show—was displayed at the Mechanics' Fair. A critic wrote:

> In vain does the carping critic declare that in the whole of God's creation neither he, nor anyone else, ever beheld those colors combined; he cannot deny that as Hill uses them, these colors harmonize perfectly with the picture as a whole. And after all, what makes a great colorist?—nothing but his peculiar power of observing contrasting, and blending colors that are passed over by the everyday beholder.[38]

However, changes detrimental to Hill's interests were in the wind. In 1893 the California School of Design became part of the San Francisco Art Association's newly constructed Mark Hopkins Institute of Art, with a credit affiliation with the University of California in Berkeley. The new trends emanating from Europe infiltrated the school, affecting the theories and examples of teachers and pupils alike. Landscapes by Thomas Hill and other painters who had ignored the new trends were considered old-fashioned.

In 1894, Hill, who kept a studio in the Flood Building, exhibited at the Art Association *Crescent Lake; Gates of the Yosemite;* and *Expectation*. All three were "For

Sale."[39] But Hill's paintings, with the exception of his sales to tourists at Wawona, did not sell.

The year 1894 was very slow for Hill. He was represented at the great California Midwinter Fair in San Francisco by only one work, *Study of Yosemite*.[40]

At the Mechanics' Fair in August Hill received what must have been a heavy blow to his prestige. William Keith was awarded the silver medal and $25 for "Best landscape painting in oil." Hill, on the other hand, won the bronze medal and $15 for the "Second best landscape in oil." The paintings Hill displayed were not new: *A Grizzly Giant; Wawona; Big Tree, Wawona; Driving the Last Spike;* and *Yosemite Valley from Inspiration Point*.[41]

While Thomas Hill had perfected a mature style that did not change through the years, William Keith, who was nine years younger than Hill, had studied continually into the 1880s. Also he had adapted his techniques to changing trends. In the 1890s his paintings were still popular; he was a wealthy man, and at the height of his powers. In the mid-1880s Keith had abandoned grand epic landscapes to paint "a clump of trees, a field, a sky."[42] He had also been influenced in 1891 toward modern trends by his eminent guest, George Inness. At the Mechanics' Fair Keith displayed *California Oaks; A Winter Moonlight in California; Early Summer Storm in Sonoma County, California; An Autumn Sunset* and *Crater Lake, Alpine County, California*.[43] Keith did not believe Yosemite *could* be painted, although he did a number of Yosemite views.

Meanwhile, Hill continued his efforts to place the

"Spike picture" at Stanford University. Leland Stanford had died in 1893; in January, 1895, Hill wrote to Mrs. Stanford and apparently placed a claim against the estate of her husband. His letter is not available, but an attorney for the estate, Frs. E. Spencer, responded, advising Hill that "The time for presenting claims has long since expired...."[44]

While vacationing at Hotel Del Coronado in San Diego, Hill received a response to a second letter he had written, this time to Attorney Spencer on January 12. The reply again contained a denial to his claim: "The estate cannot be responsible," wrote Mr. Spencer, "for the payment of your claim, and Mrs. Stanford is not individually liable therefor."[45]

In the late fall of 1895, to fulfill a commission for a painting of grand mountain scenery, Hill spent several weeks in Oregon. However, in January, 1896, harsh weather forced his return to San Francisco, where he stayed at the Palace Hotel.[46] Although, reportedly, he planned to return to Oregon and complete studies of Mount Baker,[47] it is more likely that Hill went home to Wawona, or to Raymond, where he usually wintered. At age sixty-six, it is apparent from his reduced activities that Hill's tireless energy had slowed considerably.

In August, 1896, while painting a Yosemite scene in his Wawona studio, Hill suffered the first of a series of strokes.[48] While he slowly recovered from partial paralysis, his paintings, always with price tags, were occasionally shown in San Francisco. In 1897, at the Mark Hopkins

Institute of Art, two of his paintings were displayed: *A Mountain Brook* ($300) and *White Oaks of the Plains* ($300).[49] In 1898 eight Hill paintings were displayed at the Bohemian Club with prices ranging from $250 to $500. Titles listed include five Yosemite landscapes, a New Hampshire view, and a hunting scene.[50]

A planned "comeback" for Hill was reported by the San Francisco press in July, 1899. "Again," the critic wrote, "Hill is busily painting a Yosemite landscape in his Wawona studio." A full page in the Sunday *Bulletin* was devoted to Hill and his grand Yosemite picture; a biography and a reproduction of a photograph of the artist were also included.[51]

However, the "comeback" did not actually take place, although in December Hill was reportedly working on "large Yosemite Valley scenes...to be exhibited at the opening of the new gallery in the Mark Hopkins Institute of Art." It was also noted that "first Hill plans to go to Mexico for rest and recreation."[52]

Hill did go to Mexico—where he saw a bullfight— and to other vacation areas. Excerpts from a letter written by the artist to his nephew, John Odiorne, dated May 21, 1900, describe the tours, and also reveal that Hill was indeed in a poor state of health:

My dear Nephew:
Sickness has delayed my answering your kind letter. My last three strokes of Paralysis still holds me in its grip and has put a stop to my great energy of work, in fact I have not been able to do more than keep the mill going.

But a picture from my brush I will surely send you as soon as I get fairly started again. I have not worked any to speak of for six months....

Hill continues in the letter with a description of the trips to Mexico, to Coronado—where he and his party spent two months—to Los Angeles, Santa Barbara, Del Monte, and then home to Wawona. He was traveling with a small group of relatives, including Lettie Hill, the divorced first wife of his son Edward Rufus Hill. The artist describes Lettie as his "faithful nurse through all my troubles."[53]

From 1900 through the next few years—until the 1906 earthquake in San Francisco—Hill's paintings were regularly displayed in the Art Association's annuals in the Mary Frances Searles Gallery of the Mark Hopkins Institute of Art. Sometimes only the paintings contributed to the institution by donors—*Cliff Rocks; Saco River;* and *The Golden Gate*—were shown; however, on occasion, several Hill paintings (always marked "For Sale") were added to the slim list.[54]

Although paralyzing strokes hindered the artist's efforts to paint, perception—as revealed through his correspondence—remained as clear as ever. Hill must have suffered greatly from forced inactivity. His time was spent either at Wawona or Raymond with visits to Hotel Del Coronado. Although he had difficulty in painting, his handwriting in letters to relatives and friends seems strong and steady.

In mid-May, 1903, President Theodore Roosevelt visited Yosemite Valley. Shirley Sargent describes his encounter with Thomas Hill:

> Roosevelt was there [at Wawona] but scorned a bed at the hotel in favor of sleeping on the ground beside John Muir under the Sequoias in the Mariposa Grove. However, he stopped at the hotel and charmed everyone he met. While touring Thomas Hill's studio, he admired a large painting of Bridalveil Fall, which the artist immediately gave him.[55]

On June 8, 1903, the artist's wife, Charlotte Matilda Hill, died at the age of sixty-nine in Alameda, California. On August 3, 1903, Thomas Hill's petition to claim the Piedmont Avenue, Oakland home, where his wife had lived for so many years, was granted through the efforts of his daughter, Charlotte Hill Frost.[57] However, it is not likely that the artist ever again lived in the San Francisco Bay Area.

In 1905, after Mrs. Stanford's death, Hill began corresponding with Henry C. Peterson, Curator of the Leland Stanford, Jr. Museum. Again he tried to place the "Spike picture" where he was sure it belonged—at Stanford University. At last Hill had found a sympathetic ear; Peterson agreed with the artist, and did his best to find a donor who would buy the painting and give it to the Stanford collection. Meanwhile, the painting was kept in the Golden Gate Park Memorial Museum in San Francisco, probably in storage. But in the remaining lifetime of the artist, in spite of sincere efforts on Peterson's part, a donor could not be found.[58]

Will Sparks, a San Francisco resident artist, was quoted by the press in 1906 concerning "Thomas Hill, the veteran artist of California."

> Thomas Hill is doing his work that is a puzzle to the connoisseurs who have seen it. Is it good, or is it bad? ...There seems to be something added and something lost.... Last week I saw two... impossible to believe that they were painted by the old artist of Yosemite.... Briefly, one was better than anything by Thomas Hill that I have ever seen. The other was the worst Hill I have ever seen...It all seems to please him.[59]

On June 30, 1908, in his seventy-ninth year, Thomas Hill passed away at Raymond, Madera County, California. There are indications that the artist may have taken his own life,[60] and a death certificate which could possibly settle this point, has not been located. His funeral, conducted in the Oakland home of his daughter, Adeline, was attended by representatives of the San Francisco Press Club, the Bohemian Club, the San Francisco Art Association, "and many prominent persons."[61] Burial was in Oakland's Mountain View Cemetery.[62]

VIII An End and A New Beginning

The appraisal of the artist's estate listed his personal

Fig. 24: *opposite page*
HIGH SIERRA SCENE WITH INDIANS
28½ × 48½ in.
Collection of John H. Garzoli Fine Arts.

effects and the furnishings and curios of the Wawona studio at only $157. However, in Thomas Hill's personal collection of his works at the time of his death there are listed fifty-seven oil paintings and 150 sketches, which were appraised at a total value of $44,025.50.[1]

Of great interest, also, is the fact that the paintings listed include many of Hill's major works; examples are *The Grand Canyon of the Colorado; Yosemite Valley from Inspiration Point; The Salmon Festival;* a major depiction of Muir Glacier; various large scale paintings of genre hunting and fishing scenes in landscape settings; and *The Driving of the Last Spike,* which was appraised at the highest figure: $10,000.[2]

Apparently, when the boom days ended in the eighties, Hill had withdrawn his more important pictures from auctions and had generally refused to sell them at reduced prices.

The trials of the family in attempts to dispose of the collection at acceptable prices are too myriad to discuss within the confines of this essay. Like the works of his contemporaries, Thomas Hill's paintings were not in vogue, and both he and his works remained in various degrees of obscurity for decades to come.

Finally, a permanent home was found for the "Spike picture." On December 4, 1939, a redwood tree was planted in the grounds of the E.B. Crocker Art Gallery in Sacramento on the occasion of the artist's 110th birthday and the opening of "Thomas Hill Week." The ceremonies concluded with the hanging of *The Driving of the Last Spike* in the rotunda of the California State Capitol Building.[3]

In 1954, when Paul C. Mills, Curator of the Oakland Art Gallery—which later became a department of The Oakland Museum—instigated the "California" theme for the museum's collections, the "old-fashioned" nineteenth-century paintings representing California subjects began to emerge from the decades of their obscurity—collectors scrambled to find them—and gifts to the museum's collections increased, including paintings by Hill. In 1966 the Kahn Foundation gift of money to buy paintings resulted in the acquisition of major works by Thomas Hill and paintings by many other "California" artists.

In the central court of The Oakland Museum's Gallery of California Art two grand-scale landscapes, each measuring seventy-two by one hundred and twenty inches, face each other as master works of the entire nineteenth-century scene. One painting, *Kings River Canyon,* 1878, is by William Keith. Directly opposite is one of Hill's most impressive landscapes, *Yosemite Valley (from below Sentinal Dome, as seen from Artist's Point),* 1876. Most visitors to the gallery pause to examine and enjoy these romantic grand view landscapes in their glittering gold-leafed frames. However, visitors also seem to enjoy the quiet elegance of smaller works by Thomas Hill, which are also ranked as superior paintings in the entire collection.

Notes

1. Thomas Virgil Troyon Hill, "Remarks in Fathers letters to me" (memorandum book), n.d. Archives of California Art, The Oakland Museum, gift of Cherene Holsinger and James W. Cravagan III, 1977. The definition of painting which Thomas Hill passed on to his son is a quote from a fragment by the Greek poet Simonides of Ceos (ca. 556–496 B.C.): "…poetry is vocal painting, as painting is silent poetry."

2. Paul C. Mills, unpublished manuscript, Archives of California Art, The Oakland Museum, 1967.

I Early Years

1. *Hill Family Archives;* courtesy of Mr. and Mrs. Charles C. Smith, 1979.

2. *Register:* parish of Wolverhampton, Staffordshire, England. To avoid confusion, the artist's father will henceforth be referred to as "Thomas Hill (tailor)." The subject of this biography, Thomas Hill (artist) had two sons named "Thomas": Thomas Hill, Jr., who died in infancy, and Thomas Virgil Troyon Hill; the latter further confused the records by occasionally using the appendage, "Jr."

3. *Hill Family Archives.*

4. *Hill Family Letters, 1844–1861;* courtesy of Mr. and Mrs. Howard F. Lea and Mr. and Mrs. Charles C. Smith.

5. *Hill Family Archives.*

6. *Ibid.*

7. "Smethcott" (Victoria Survey), *A County History of Shropshire*, n.d., p. 160.

8. Mrs. C. W. Hill (Oakland, Calif.), letter to Mabel R. Gillis (California State Library, Sacramento), February, 1940.

9. Thomas Hill (tailor—New York City), letter to Edward Kidd (Birmingham, England), October 8, 1843.

10. *Ibid.*

11. *Wolverhampton Registers* (birth certificates): "9 Dec 1843 at The Union Poor House, Wolverhampton. EDWARD, son of Thomas & MARIA (HUNT) HILL—Tailor." Edward Hill, whose death date is not established, spent most of his adult life as a landscape painter in New England. Since he visited his brother Thomas in California and painted California landscapes, he is frequently confused with his nephew, brother Thomas' son, Edward Rufus Hill (1852–1908), who also became a "California" painter.

12. Thomas Hill (tailor—Taunton, Mass.), letter to his brother, Francis Hill (Wolverhampton), August 25, 1844.

13. *Ibid.*

14. Thomas Hill (tailor—Taunton), letter to Edward Kidd (Birmingham, England), February 2, [1845].

15. *Ibid.*, July 27, 1845.

16. Thomas Hill (tailor—Taunton), letter to "Dear Brother" (England), April 25, 1847.

17. *Ibid.*, November 11, 1847.

18. Vital Statistics Bureau, State House, Boston, Mass. Maria Hunt Hill had borne ten children but not all lived to maturity. Circa 1852 Thomas Hill (tailor) married his second wife, Margaret Allen Hill (1813–1866); they had one child, a daughter, Maria Allen Hill.

19. *Ibid.* Thomas Hill (artist) and his wife had eleven children; nine lived to maturity.

20. Robert H. Fletcher, *Memorandum of Artists*, 1906, p. 3. California State Library, Sacramento.

21. Catherine Stover (Pennsylvania Academy of the Fine Arts), letter to Marjorie Arkelian (The Oakland Museum), March 29, 1979.

22. Taken from the inscription on the original silver medal; information courtesy of William C. Frost.

Fig. 25: FLOWERS IN A WINDOW
36 × 20 in.
Collection of The Oakland Museum
Gift of the Kahn Foundation.

Fig. 26: *opposite page*
STILL LIFE WITH DUCKS AND VEGETABLES
27 × 33 in.
Collection of The Fine Arts Museums of San Francisco
Gift of A. H. Brawner.

23. *Benjamin Champney's Guest Books;* information courtesy of Phyllis F. Greene, 1979.

24. Phyllis F. Greene (North Conway, N.H.), letter to Marjorie Arkelian, July 16, 1979.

25. Dorothy McCullough Lee (Portland, Ore.), letter to Marjorie Arkelian, August 27, 1979.

26. Benjamin Champney, *Sixty Years' Memories of Art and Artists* (Woburn, Mass.: The News Print, Wallace & Andrew, 1900).

27. *Ibid.*, pp. 145–146.

28. Heywood-Wakefield Company, "Invitation to Market," Chicago, July 6–24, 1926. Archives of California Art, The Oakland Museum, gift of Cherene Holsinger and James W. Cravagan III, 1977

29. *Ibid.* Items of furniture decorated by the Hill brothers still exist in private ownerships.

30. Benjamin Hill (East Boston), letter to "Dear Father and Mother" (England), April 13, 1861.

II California 1861–1866

1. *Pioneer Records for Thomas Hill*, California State Library, Sacramento, February, 1940.

2. James de T. Abajian, California Artists Card Catalogue, San Francisco, 1969–1979.

3. San Francisco City Directories, 1862–1864; the artist's dwelling is listed in those years as "South side of Folsom between 7th and 8th Sts."

4. Wawona Washburn Hartwig (Beverly Hills, Calif.), letter with Hill family chronological listings, to Marjorie Arkelian, March 21, 1979.

5. William E. Colby (ed.), "Notes and Correspondence," *Sierra Club Bulletin* (San Francisco), Vol. X, no. 3 (1918), 340–343.

6. Mechanics' Institute and Library of San Francisco, *Industrial Exhibition Report*, 1864.

7. *The Elevator* (San Francisco), July 21, 1865, p. 2, col. 4.

8. California Art Union, *A Classified Catalogue of the Paintings on Exhibition*, San Francisco, 1865.

9. *The Elevator, loc. cit.*

10. *Ibid*. Through lack of funds the California Art Union failed; some of the artists blamed the purchase of Hill's painting for the failure.

11. Benjamin Parke Avery, "Art Beginnings on the Pacific," *The Overland Monthly* (San Francisco), Vol. I, no. 2 (August, 1868), 113–114.

12. *Ibid*.

13. Charles C. Dobie, *San Francisco's Chinatown* (New York: D. Appleton-Century Company, 1936), p. 79.

14. Hans Huth, "Yosemite, the Story of an Idea," *Sierra Club Bulletin*, Vol. XXXIII, no. 3 (March, 1948), 47–78.

III Paris 1866–1867

1. Robert H. Fletcher, *Memorandum of Artists*, 1906, p. 3.

2. Maria Naylor (ed.), *The National Academy of Design Exhibition Record. 1861–1890* (2 vols., New York: Kennedy Galleries, Inc., 1973), Vol. I, p. 439. This painting is currently in the collection of The New-York Historical Society.

3. *Pioneer Records for Thomas Hill*, California State Library, Sacramento.

4. Flora Hill McCullough, "Memoirs" (unpublished manuscript), Archives of California Art, The Oakland Museum, 1962.

5. *Ibid.*

6. *Ibid.*

7. *Transcript* (Boston), February 24, 1868.

8. *Ibid.*

9. McCullough, *op. cit.* According to Flora Hill McCullough, her sister, Estella Louise, was named after Princess Louise.

10. "Thomas Hill, Artist," *The Argonaut* (San Francisco), December 12, 1908, p. 406.

IV New England 1867–1871

1. Yosemite National Park Research Center; information courtesy of Maud Lindemann, Madera County Historical Society, Madera, Calif., 1979.

2. "An Hour with the Artists," *Transcript* (Boston), January 27, 1868.

3. "The Yo-Semite Valley by Mr. Thomas Hill," *Transcript* (Boston), February 24, 1868.

4. *Ibid.*

5. "Art Items," *Transcript* (Boston), March 18, 1868.

6. *Transcript* (Boston), June 17, 1868.

7. B. P. Avery, "Art Beginnings on the Pacific," *The Overland Monthly*, Vol. I, no. 2 (August, 1868), 113–114.

8. *Transcript* (Boston), *loc. cit.* The sketches for the painting were taken by Hill during his sojourn in California from 1861 to 1866, as previously noted.

9. Katharine M. McClinton, *The Chromolithographs of Louis Prang* (New York: Clarkson N. Potter, Inc., 1973), p. 11.

10. Charles H. Brainard, "The Early Home of Whittier," *The Ramrod* (Haverhill, Mass., June, 1869, reprinted from the *New York Independent*, n.d.).

11. *Transcript* (Boston), November 10, 1868.

12. *Catalogue of Pictures on Exhibition at Snow & Roos Art Gallery*, April, 1869. Archives of California Art, The Oakland Museum. Hill may have spent weeks or months sketching and painting in the White Mountains in 1869.

13. *Transcript* (Boston), December 7, 1870.

14. *Ibid.*, November 28, 1923.

15. *Ibid.*, December 7, 1870.

16. By 1870 Keith was a full-fledged painter in San Francisco specializing in landscape.

17. *Alta California* (San Francisco), March 27, 1870.

18. Wawona Washburn Hartwig (Beverly Hills), letter to Marjorie Arkelian, September 18, 1978.

V California and the Art Boom of the 1870s

1. Kent L. Seavey, *Artist-Teachers & Pupils; San Francisco Art Association and California School of Design, the First Fifty Years, 1871–1921* (exhibition catalogue), California Historical Society, June 1–September 4, 1971.

2. *Elite Directory* (San Francisco), 1879, pp. 141–142.

3. Jack Jackson (Boston Athenaeum), letter to George W. Neubert (The Oakland Museum), May 24, 1979.

4. Yosemite National Park Research Center. It is said that Hill acquired thirty-one medals and awards in his career. The Palette Club medal is located; information courtesy of William C. Frost.

Fig. 27: VIEW OF YOSEMITE, 1864
36 × 56 in.
Collection of the Los Angeles County Museum of Art
William Randolph Hearst Collection.

5. This painting was probably destroyed in the San Francisco earthquake and fire of 1906.

6. Research archives of the Crocker Art Museum, Sacramento; information courtesy of Richard V. West.

7. *San Francisco Art Association Catalogue* (second exhibition), 1872. Archives of California Art, The Oakland Museum.

8. *Souvenir Catalogue of the Annual Exhibition of Works by the Artist Members of the Bohemian Club, 1872–1947*, San Francisco, May 2–17, 1947.

9. Boston Art Club, *Fine Arts Exhibition*, January, 1873.

10. Jackson, *op. cit.*

11. *Catalogue of Fine Oil Paintings Offered at Private Competitive Sale, by Elliot, Blakeslee & Noyes*, Boston, May, 1873.

12. *San Francisco Art Association Catalogue* (fourth exhibition), 1873. Archives of California Art, The Oakland Museum. Hill painted more than one version of *The Royal Arches*; later displays, perhaps of other versions, evoked favorable press reviews.

13. *Ibid.*

14. *News Letter* (San Francisco), November 1, 1873.

15. *Bulletin* (San Francisco), December 10, 1873.

16. *Chronicle* (San Francisco), December 12, 1873.

17. Harry Mulford, "A History of the San Francisco Art Institute Artists and Men" (Calendar of Events), March, 1973.

18. Marjorie Wright, "Officers and Teachers of the San Francisco Art Association, 1871–1967" (research report), Archives of California Art, The Oakland Museum.

19. *Archives of the Bohemian Club*, San Francisco, January 29, 1962.

20. Flora Hill McCullough, "Memoirs" (unpublished manuscript), Archives of California Art, The Oakland Museum, 1962. A third son, Robert Rembrandt Hill, who often accompanied his father on sketching tours, became a San Francisco printer.

21. Mechanics' Institute and Library of San Francisco, *Industrial Exhibition Report*, 1874.

22. *Chronicle* (San Francisco), November 8, 1874.

23. *Alta California* (San Francisco), January 8, 1875.

24. *Ibid.*, January 22, 1875.

25. "Art Notes," *The Overland Monthly*, Vol. XIII, no. 5 (November, 1874), 485–486.

26. *News Letter* (San Francisco), July 24, 1875.

27. *Ibid.*, July 31, 1875.

28. *Bulletin* (San Francisco), May 1, 1875.

29. *News Letter* (San Francisco), January 1, 1876.

30. *Ibid.*, January 15, 1876.

31. Clara E. Clement and Laurence Hutton, *Artists of the Nineteenth Century* (revised ed., 1884; reprint ed., St. Louis, Mo.: North Point, Inc., 1969), pp. 356–357.

32. *Post* (San Francisco), April 13, 1876, p. 6.

33. *News Letter* (San Francisco), May 27, 1876.

34. San Francisco City Directories, 1876; 1877–1878; 1878–1879.

35. Mechanics' Institute and Library of San Francisco, *Industrial Exposition Report*, 1864, p. 224.

Fig. 28: YOSEMITE VALLEY, 1867
26¼ × 42½ in.
Private collection.

36. "Painter and Palette—Thomas Hill," *Chronicle* (San Francisco), April 22, 1877.

37. *The Argonaut* (San Francisco), April 15, 1877.

38. *Chronicle* (San Francisco), June 3, 1877.

39. *Marin Journal* (San Rafael, Calif.), June 7, 1877.

40. *Post* (San Francisco), *ca.* August 7, 1877.

41. The medals have been located; information courtesy of William C. Frost.

42. The Mechanics' Institute and Library of San Francisco, *Industrial Exhibition Report*, 1877.

43. Theophilus d'Estrella, "Virgil Williams' Art Notes to a Deaf-Mute Pupil," *The Overland Monthly*, Vol. IX, no. 51 (new series, March, 1887), 286.

VI California 1879–1884

1. San Francisco City Directory, 1879.

2. *Indenture:* C.B. Elliott to Charlotte M. Hill, March 5, 1879. Alameda County Records, Oakland, Calif. The northerly part of the Hill estate was located in what is now the southerly extension of the Mills College campus.

3. *Transactions of the California State Agricultural Society*, Sacramento, 1879.

4. *San Francisco Art Association catalogue* (spring exhibition), 1880.

5. *The Jewish Times* (San Francisco), March 5, 1880.

6. *Chronicle* (San Francisco), May 9, 1880. *The Driving of the Last Spike* was unfinished at this time.

7. Phyllis F. Greene (North Conway, N.H.), letter to Rudolph Wunderlich (Kennedy Galleries, N.Y.), August 5, 1969; information courtesy of Kennedy Galleries.

8. *Chronicle* (San Francisco), October 3, 1880, p. 5.

9. *Examiner* (San Francisco), November 28, 1880.

10. *Alta California* (San Francisco), January 29, 1881.

11. *News Letter* (San Francisco), February 12, 1881.

12. For Thomas Hill's own description of the painting see the booklet he is alleged to have written—and did copyright in 1881—*The Last Spike, a Painting by Thomas Hill* (San Francisco: E. Bosqui & Co., January, 1881). The unique booklet, written in the third person, contains Hill's key to the portraits, which include four women, and attempts to justify the inclusion of individuals who were not actually present at the ceremony. See also Thomas Hill, *History of the 'Spike Picture' and why it is Still in my Possession* (pamphlet), published by Thomas Hill (thirty copies privately distributed), 1884.

13. Hill did not have a commission in writing—from all accounts—however, he did have every reason to rely on a verbal agreement. The exact terms of any verbal agreement between him and Stanford vary according to the source. The painting was still owned by the artist at the time of his death in 1908.

14. Adeline Matilda Hill, interviewed by Theodore Baggelmann (mail questionnaire), August, 1941. When the artist's children had families of their own they frequently called their father, Thomas Hill, "grandfather."

15. *Chronicle* (San Francisco), April 3, 1881.

16. *Ibid.*

17. *White Mountain Echo* (Bethlehem, N.H.), July 30, 1881, p. 12.

18. Charles Vogel (Townsend Harbor, Mass.), letter to Marjorie Arkelian, October 1, 1978.

19. *Transactions of the California State Agricultural Society*, 1881.

20. Mechanics' Institute and Library of San Francisco, *Industrial Exhibition Report*, 1881.

21. *Call* (San Francisco), March 10, 1882, p. 3, col. 6.

22. *Ibid.*

23. Wawona Washburn Hartwig (Beverly Hills), letter to Marjorie Arkelian, September 18, 1978.

24. Mechanics' Institute and Library of San Francisco, *Industrial Exhibition Report*, 1882.

25. Yosemite National Park Research Center; information courtesy of Mary Vocelka, 1980. Charles Dormon Robinson (1847–1933), also a "California" painter, had a studio next door to "the Guardian's" home. Robinson had opened the studio in 1880, and came every summer to the Valley for twenty-four years. However, he is best known in retrospect as a marine painter. Both Hill and Robinson, however, sold paintings to hundreds of visitors to Yosemite, including royalty.

26. *New Letter* (San Francisco), July 28, 1883, p. 5.

27. Mechanics' Institute and Library of San Francisco, *Industrial Exhibition Report*, 1883.

28. *Chronicle* (San Francisco), December 29, 1883, p. 3, col. 9.

29. The medal is located; information courtesy of William C. Frost. For a description of the Temple Awards see Pennsylvania Academy of the Fine Arts, *Catalogue of the Sixty-Sixth Annual Exhibition*, Philadelphia, 1897, which also lists all gold and silver Temple Award winners.

30. *Herald* (Boston), May 25, 1884.

VII The Yosemite Years 1884–1908

1. Shirley Sargent, *Yosemite's Historic Wawona* (Yosemite: Flying Spur Press, 1979) p. 39.

2. *Argonaut* (San Francisco), August 23, 1884, p. 6.

3. *San Franciscan*, Vol. III, no. 2 (January 31, 1885), p. 13.

4. Theresa D. Cederholm (Boston Public Library), letter to Marjorie Arkelian, April 4, 1979.

5. *Call* (San Francisco), April 28, 1885, p. 3, col. 6.

6. *Indenture:* Thomas Hill et al to Metha A. Nelson, February 24, 1886. Alameda County Records, Oakland.

7. *Declaration of Homestead*, Charlotte M. Hill (wife of Thomas Hill), March 1, 1887. Alameda County Records, Oakland.

8. Elizabeth H. Godfrey, "Thomas Hill," *Yosemite Nature Notes*, Vol. XXIII, no. 3 (March, 1944), 30–31.

9. "A Week of Art," *Post* (San Francisco), May 1, 1886, p. 1, col. 6.

10. Vital Statistics Bureau, State House, Boston, 1886.

11. *White Mountain Echo* (Bethlehem, N.H.), August 7, 1886.

12. *San Francisco Art Association Minutes—March 21, 1871–August 29, 1889;* information courtesy of the San Francisco Art Institute, 1966.

13. *Call* (San Francisco), December 22, 1886, p. 5, col. 4.

14. *Ibid.*

15. Richard R. Hanna, interviewed by George W. Neubert and Marjorie Arkelian, The Oakland Museum, December 16, 1977.

16. Information courtesy of Christine Reid (Cambridge, Mass.), 1979.

17. The original letter is located in the Holt-Atherton Pacific Center for Western Studies at the University of the Pacific, Stockton, Calif.

18. John Muir (ed.), *Picturesque California* (2 vols., New York and San Francisco: J. Dewing and Co., 1888).

19. James Mason Hutchings, *In the Heart of the Sierras* (Oakland, Calif: Pacific Press Publishing House, 1888). In 1855 Hutchings had taken the first artist into Yosemite, Thomas A. Ayres, who made the first published Yosemite views. The 1888 book is mainly a compilation from earlier issues of *Hutchings' Illustrated California Magazine* published in San Francisco by Hutchings and Rosenfeld. Many illustrations are reproductions from depictions by Charles and Arthur Nahl and other artists, with credits frequently omitted.

20. Mechanics' Institute and Library of San Francisco, *Industrial Exhibit Report*, 1888.

21. Thomas Hill, letter to "Hon. Leland Stanford," November 22, 1889; courtesy of Theodore Baggelmann, Sacramento, 1979.

22. *San Francisco Art Association Catalogue*, May, 1890.

23. *Daily Record Union* (Sacramento), September 19, 1890.

24. Shirley Sargent, *op. cit.* (see note 1).

25. *San Francisco Art Association Catalogue*, May, 1891.

26. For an account of Inness in California, see Marjorie Arkelian and George W. Neubert, *George Inness Landscapes: His Signature Years 1884–1894* (exhibition catalogue), The Oakland Museum, November 28, 1978–January 28, 1979.

27. Thomas Virgil Troyon Hill, "Remarks in Fathers letters to me" (memorandum book), n.d. Archives of California Art, The Oakland Museum, gift of Cherene Holsinger and James W. Cravagan III, 1977.

28. *Chronicle* (San Francisco), October 4, 1891.

29. *White Mountain Echo* (Bethlehem, N.H.), August, 1892.

30. *Call* (San Francisco), December 12, 1892, p. 8.

31. *The Wave* (San Francisco), Vol. X, no. 3 (January 21, 1893), 3.

32. Adeline Matilda Hill, interviewed by Theodore Baggelmann (mail questionnaire), August, 1941. The candid remarks concerning the artist's temperamental outbursts are interesting because equally reliable sources refer to Hill's disposition as kindly and genial, which it would seem he was, most of the time.

33. *Final Report, California at the World's Columbian Exposition, Chicago, 1893.* Sacramento State Office, 1894, pp. 53, 168.

34. Thomas Hill (diary notes in Bank of California passbook), 1893; courtesy of Theodore Baggelmann, 1979.

35. *Ibid.*

36. Thomas Virgil Troyon Hill, "Remarks in Fathers letters to me" (memorandum book), n. d. The Oakland Museum, gift of Cherene Holsinger and James W. Cravagan III, 1977.

37. Thomas Hill, diary notes (see note 34).

38. "The True Line. Some Notable Work of California Artists," *Call* (San Francisco), May 28, 1893, p. 26, col. 3.

39. San Francisco Art Association, *Mark Hopkins Institute of Art Catalogue* (spring exhibition), 1893.

40. *Catalogue of the California Midwinter International Exposition*, 1894.

41. Mechanics' Institute and Library of San Francisco, *Industrial Exhibition Report*, 1894.

42. Bro. Cornelius F.S.C., M.A., *Keith: Old Master of California* (New York: G.P. Putnam's Sons, 1942), p. 82.

43. Mechanics' Institute, *op. cit.*

44. Frs. E. Spencer, letter to Thomas Hill (San Francisco), January 8, 1895; courtesy of Theodore Baggelmann, 1979.

45. Frs. E. Spencer (San Jose, Calif.), letter to Thomas Hill (Coronado Beach, Calif.), January 26, 1895; courtesy of Theodore Baggelmann, 1979.

Fig. 29: VIRGIL WILLIAMS' CABIN NEAR ST. HELENA
14¾ × 22¼ in.
Collection of The Oakland Museum, gift of Mrs. Samuel Kahn and Mrs. Walter Mayer in memory of their parents, Joseph and Harriet Weissbein.

46. *Chronicle* (San Francisco), January 11, 1896.

47. *Ibid.*

48. "Thomas Hill at the Door of Death" (unsourced article), August 19, 1896.

49. San Francisco Art Association, *Mark Hopkins Institute of Art Catalogue* (winter exhibition), 1897.

50. The Bohemian Club, *Exhibition of Paintings* (catalogue), San Francisco, 1898.

51. *Bulletin* (San Francisco), July 16, 1899, Part III, p. 17.

52. San Francisco Art Association, *Mark Hopkins Institute Review of Art*, Vol. I, no. 1 (December, 1899).

53. Thomas Hill (Wawona, Calif.), letter to John Odiorne, May 21, 1900; courtesy of Mrs. Donald Wood, 1979. "Lettie" (Willeta Smith Hill) and the artist's daughter, Estella Washburn, nursed Hill at Wawona through the illnesses of his last years.

54. For listings and dates see Mark Hopkins Institute of Art exhibition catalogues (1900–1905).

55. Shirley Sargent, *Yosemite's Historic Wawona* (Yosemite: Flying Spur Press, 1979), p. 58.

56. Records of the Township of Oakland, Alameda County Courthouse, 1903.

57. *Petition:* Thomas Hill, in the Superior Court of the County of Alameda, State of California, August 3, 1903.

58. *Biographical Letter File* (Hill-Peterson), California State Library, Sacramento.

59. Will Sparks, "The Puzzling Work of Thomas Hill, the Painter of the Yosemite Valley," *Call* (San Francisco), September 9, 1906, p. 27.

60. George A. Groce and David H. Wallace, *The New-York Historical Society's Dictionary of Artists in America 1564–1860* (New Haven: Yale University Press, 1957), p. 317.

61. Wawona Washburn Hartwig, *op. cit.*

62. Archives of the Mountain View Cemetery, Oakland, Calif.

VIII *An End and a New Beginning*

1. *Catalogue of the Paintings and Sketches by the Late Thomas Hill*, collection on exhibition and sale by Robert R. Hill, Administrator. Exhibition Gallery, San Francisco, (December, 1910).

2. *Ibid.*

3. *Union* (Sacramento), December 5, 1939, p. 9, col. 1.

Chronology

1829	*Sept. 11:* Thomas Hill born in Birmingham, England.
1829–1843	Probably attends local day schools or is taught at home in Smethcott, Salop County, and in Wolverhampton.
1835	Begins to experiment with oil painting, which becomes a continued endeavor.
1843	Remains in Wolverhampton while father (a tailor) seeks "constant employment" in United States.
1844	*July 8:* Voyages steerage with mother, brothers and sisters, to join father in New York City. Reunited family settles in Taunton, Mass. Works in cotton factory. Not required to go to school although it is state law.
1845–1846	Works as carriage painter. Also decorates furniture.
1847	Leaves Taunton to work for interior decorators in Boston.
1851	*Nov. 16:* Marries Charlotte Matilda Hawkes in Boston.
1853	Enrolls in life class under Peter Frederick Rothermel at Pennsylvania Academy of the Fine Arts. Wins silver medal and membership in Graphic

	Club for fruit and flower study entered at Maryland Institute exhibition.
1854	Paints in White Mountains, N.H., with Benjamin Champney.
1855	Moves to Cambridge, Mass. Two of three children die in infancy.
1855–1858	Active in Boston. Paints in White Mountains with group including Champney, Durand, Inness, Bierstadt, Virgil Williams.
1858	Makes home in Chelsea, Mass.
1859–1860	Decorates furniture for Heywood-Wakefield Company in Gardner, Mass.
1861	Health threatened. Travels overland with wife and children seeking warmer climate in California. Settles in San Francisco.
1862	Listed as "portrait painter." Makes first trip to Yosemite with Virgil Williams and William Keith.
1863	Paints Russian River and Yosemite landscapes.
1864	Sketches in Sierra Nevada mountains. Exhibits portraits, landscapes, and sketches in San Francisco.

1865   Sells *Trial Scene from the Merchant of Venice* to California Art Union for $700 in gold. Executes large landscapes for public houses in San Francisco.

1866   Exhibits *View of the Yo-Semite Valley in California* at National Academy of Design in New York City. Studies six months in Paris with German painter Paul Meyerheim. Persuaded by Meyerheim to specialize in landscape.

1867   Exhibits at Paris Universal Exposition.

1868–1870   Listed in Boston: Thomas Hill, artist; 49 Studio Building, house at Cambridge. Very active in Boston.
1868: Paints and exhibits *"The Yo-Semite Valley, ten by six feet,"* in Boston, from sketches taken in California.;
Paints *Whittier's Birthplace*.
1870: Paints *The Wayside Inn*, which is chromolithographed by Louis Prang & Co. Louis Prang buys original painting.

1871   Health fails again. Returns with family to San Francisco via Isthmus of Panama. Helps to organize San Francisco Art Association.
Wins bronze medal for *Great Canyon of the Sierras*, 1871, exhibited at Palette Club, New York City.

1872   Sells *Great Canyon of the Sierras*, 1871, to Judge E.B. Crocker of Sacramento. Sells famed *Yo-Semite Valley*, 1868, to railroad magnate Charles Crocker of San Francisco.
Summer: Guest of Virgil Williams at the latter's cabin retreat in Sonoma Valley. Gathers sketches for paintings.

1873–1874   Joins San Francisco Bohemian Club. Keeps Boston contacts active. Exhibits in San Francisco. Recognized as "an artist of eminence."

1875   Becomes a partner in Joseph Roos' San Francisco art store.
Travels east to buy paintings for the store's "Beaux-Arts Gallery."
Sells paintings for high prices. Reportedly averages $20,000 annually from sales.

1876   Buys out Joseph Roos & Co. in San Francisco. Renames business "Thomas Hill & Co."—keeps Beaux-Arts Gallery functioning.
Wins bronze medal at Centennial Exposition, Philadelphia.

1877   Begins sketching for *The Driving of the Last Spike* (1881), a painting suggested by Leland Stanford, depicting the ceremony honoring the completion in 1869 of the transcontinental railroad at Promontory Point, Utah.

Fig. 30: OUR CAMP
12 × 18 in.
Collection of The Oakland Museum
Gift of the Kahn Foundation.

1877–1878 Participates in San Francisco and Boston exhibitions.

1879 Sells San Francisco gallery to Snow & Company. Listed in San Francisco as "landscape and marine painter," studio at 1227 Turk Street.
Buys twenty-room house on ten-acre lot in Seminary Park, Oakland.
Exhibits locally and wins gold medal at state fair, although economic depression curtails sales.

1880 *Summer:* Paints in White Mountains with brother, landscape painter Edward Hill.

1881 Forced to accept rejection by Leland Stanford of *The Last Spike*, which is exhibited in San Francisco and in Sacramento.

1882 Auctions large collection of paintings which bring low prices.
Withdraws best works from sale.
Summer: In Yosemite Valley.

1883 Builds studio in Yosemite Valley. Exhibits Yosemite landscapes in San Francisco.
Dec.: Takes part in first auction sale at San Francisco Art Association. Paintings bring low prices.

1884 Wins coveted Temple Medal for a Yosemite landscape exhibited at Pennsylvania Academy of the Fine Arts annual.

Summer: Finds studio in Yosemite Valley demolished by windstorm. Stays at Wawona Hotel twenty-five miles south of Yosemite.
Aug.: Sketches and paints in Yellowstone Park area.
Winter: Visits New Orleans. Returns to Boston area.

1885 *April:* Attends wedding at Hill residence in Oakland of daughter Estella Louise to John Stephen Washburn, a proprietor of Wawona Hotel.

1886 Forced to sell heavily mortgaged Oakland estate. Keeps San Francisco studio and exhibits in California but lives at Wawona Hotel. Establishes studio next door to Wawona Hotel. Sells paintings to tourists.
Fall: Paints in White Mountains with Champney.
Dec.: Volunteers to take place of Virgil Williams (deceased) as director of San Francisco Art Association's California School of Design—without compensation—until replacement can be found.

1887 Abandons directorship when commissioned by naturalist John Muir to paint Muir Glacier, Alaska. Travels by steamboat to Alaska.
Keeps studio in San Francisco but lives at Wawona. Wife lives in Oakland.

1888 Nineteen Hill landscapes reproduced in *Picturesque California*.

PHOTOGRAPH OF THOMAS HILL'S STUDIO IN YOSEMITE
Collection of The Oakland Museum
Gift of Cherene Holsinger and James W. Cravagan III.

PHOTOGRAPH OF THE INTERIOR OF THOMAS HILL'S
STUDIO IN YOSEMITE
Collection of The Oakland Museum
Gift of Cherene Holsinger and James W. Cravagan III.

	Wins premium award at Mechanics' Institute Fair in San Francisco.
1889	Exhibits in San Francisco and Sacramento but spends most of year at Wawona. Writes to Leland Stanford requesting that "the Last Spike" should find a new home at Stanford University.
1890–1891	Wins gold medal at State Fair. Exhibits in San Francisco. Resides at Wawona and Raymond, Calif.
1892	*Summer:* Paints in White Mountains with brother Edward. At Wawona prepares for coming World's Columbian Exposition in Chicago.
1893	Travels by train to Chicago to see Exposition which includes several of his major works. Keeps diary.
1894	In San Francisco keeps studio in Flood Building. Exhibits locally but paintings do not sell. In California Midwinter International Exposition exhibits only a study of Yosemite. *Aug.:* Awarded bronze medal at Mechanics' Fair for "second best landscape in oil."
1895	Attempts to place claim against estate of Leland Stanford for payment for "Spike picture." Claim rejected.

1896	*Aug.:* At Wawona studio suffers first of a series of strokes.
1896–1898	Activities and painting drastically curtailed.
1899	A planned "comeback" supported by extensive San Francisco press coverage does not materialize.
1900	Writes to nephew, John Odiorne, describing three strokes of paralysis, and extensive vacation trips to Mexico, Coronado Beach, Monterey, and San Francisco. Returns to permanent residence at Wawona and Raymond.
1903	*May:* Gives President Theodore Roosevelt, a guest at the Wawona Hotel, a large painting of "Bridalveil Fall," which Roosevelt admired in his studio.
1905	Again thwarted in attempts to place the "Spike picture" at Stanford University.
1905–1908	Inactive. Requires constant care.
1908	*June 30:* Dies at Raymond.

Selected Bibliography

Books

Art in California. San Francisco: R.L. Bernier, 1916.

Bancroft, Hubert Howe. *Retrospection: Political and Personal*. New York: The Bancroft Company, 1912.

Barker, Virgil. *American Painting: History and Interpretation*. New York: The Macmillan Company, 1950.

Benjamin, Samuel Greene Wheeler. *Art in America: A Critical and Historical Sketch*. New York: Harper & Brothers, 1880.

_____. *Our American Artists*. Second series. Boston: D. Lothrop & Co., 1881.

California World's Fair Commission. *Final Report, California at the World's Columbian Exposition, Chicago, 1893*. Sacramento: State Printing, 1894.

Champney, Benjamin. *Sixty Years' Memories of Art and Artists*. Woburn, Massachusetts: The News Print, Wallace & Andrews, 1900.

Clark, George T. *Leland Stanford*. Stanford, California: Stanford University Press, 1931.

Cornelius, Brother. *Keith: Old Master of California*. New York: G.P. Putnam's Sons, 1942.

Cummins, Ella Sterling. *The Story of the Files*. San Francisco: The World's Fair Commission, 1893.

Dobie, Charles Caldwell. *San Francisco's Chinatown*. New York: D. Appleton-Century Company, 1936.

Fletcher, Robert H. (ed.). *The Annals of the Bohemian Club, 1887–1895*. Vol. III. San Francisco: The Bohemian Club, 1909.

Freeman, Dr. Larry. *Louis Prang: Color Lithographer*. Watkins Glen, New York: Century House, 1971.

Getlein, Frank. *The Lure of the Great West*. Waukesha, Wisconsin: Country Beautiful, 1973.

Greene, Clay M. (ed.). *The Annals of the Bohemian Club, 1895–1906*. Vol. IV. San Francisco: The Bohemian Club, 1930.

Hailey, Gene (ed.). *California Art Research Monographs*. San Francisco: Works Progress Administration, 1937.

Hartmann, Sadakichi. *A History of American Art*. Vol. I (of 2). Boston: L.C. Page & Company, 1901.

Hitchings, Sinclair. " 'Fine Art Lithography' in Boston: Craftsmanship in Color, 1840–1900." *Art and Commerce: American Prints of the Nineteenth Century*. Boston: Museum of Fine Arts, 1978.

Hittell, John S. *A Guide Book to San Francisco*. San Francisco: The Bancroft Company, 1888.

Hutchings, James Mason. *In the Heart of the Sierras*. Oakland, California: Pacific Press Publishing House, 1888.

Fig. 31: UNTITLED LANDSCAPE, 1872
36 × 60 in.
Collection of John H. Garzoli Fine Arts.

Photograph by Lee Fatherree.

_____. *Scenes of Wonder and Curiosity in California: Guide to the Yo-Semite Valley*. New York: A. Roman and Company, 1870.

Levy, Florence N. (ed.). *American Art Annual*. Washington, D.C.: The American Federation of Arts, VII (1909–1910).

Lick, Rosemary. *The Generous Miser*. Los Angeles: Ward Ritchie Press, 1967.

Lloyd, Benjamin Estell. *Lights and Shades in San Francisco*. San Francisco: A.L. Bancroft & Co., 1876.

McClinton, Katharine Morrison. *The Chromolithographs of Louis Prang*. New York: Clarkson N. Potter, Inc., 1973.

Moore, Esther Gilman. *History of Gardner Massachusetts, 1785–1967*. Gardner: Hatton Printing, Inc., 1967.

Muir, John. *Travels in Alaska*. Boston: Houghton Mifflin Company, 1915.

_____. *Picturesque California: The Rocky Mountains and the Pacific Slope*. 2 vols. New York: J. Dewing Publishing Co., 1888.

Naylor, Maria (ed.). *The National Academy of Design Exhibition Record, 1861–1900*. Vol. I (of 2). New York: Kennedy Galleries, Inc., 1973.

Neuhaus, Eugen. *The History and Ideals of American Art*. Stanford, California: Stanford University Press, 1931.

Neville, Amelia Ransome. *The Fantastic City*. Boston: Houghton Mifflin Company, 1932.

Paris, William Francklyn. *The Hall of American Artists*. 10 vols. New York: New York University, IX (1954).

Peters, Harry Twyford. *America on Stone*. Garden City, New York: Doubleday, Doran and Company, Inc., 1931.

Putnam, Eben. *Lieutenant Joshua Hewes*. New York: privately printed, 1913.

Richardson, Edgar P. *American Romantic Painting*. New York: E. Weyhe, 1944.

Russell, Carl Purcher. *One Hundred Years in Yosemite*. Berkeley: University of California Press, 1947.

Sargent, Shirley. *Yosemite's Historic Wawona*. Yosemite: Flying Spur Press, 1979.

Sears, Clara Endicott. *Highlights Among the Hudson River Artists*. Boston: Houghton Mifflin Company, 1947.

Taft, Robert. *Artists and Illustrators of the Old West*. New York: Charles Scribner's Sons, 1953.

Taylor, Mrs. H.J. *Yosemite Indians and Other Sketches*. San Francisco: Johnck & Seeger, 1936.

Tuckerman, Henry T. *Book of the Artists*. 2d ed. New York: James F. Carr, 1966.

Dictionaries and Encyclopedias

Bénézit, E. *Dictionnaire critique et documentaire des Peintres, Sculpteurs, Dessinateurs et Graveurs*. Vol. V. Nouvelle édition. Paris: Librairie Gründ, 1976.

Champlin, John D., Jr. and Perkins, Charles C. *Cyclopedia of Painters and Paintings*. Vol. II. New York: Charles Scribner's Sons, 1913.

Clement, Clara Erskine and Hutton, Laurence. *Artists of the Nineteenth Century and Their Works*. Vol. I (of 2). Boston: Houghton, Mifflin and Company, 1880.

Groce, George C. and Wallace, David H. *The New-York Historical Society's Dictionary of Artists in America, 1564–1860*. New Haven, Connecticut: Yale University Press, 1957.

Malone, Dumas (ed.). *Dictionary of American Biography*. Vol. V. New York: Charles Scribner's Sons, 1964.

Thieme, Ulrich and Becker, Felix. *Allgemeines Lexikon der bildenden Künstler*. Vol. XVII. Leipzig: E.A. Seemann, 1931.

Exhibition Catalogues

Administrator's Sale, Valuable and Historical Paintings, to Close the Estate of the Late Thomas Hill, the Great American Painter. Sutter Street Salesrooms, San Francisco, [November, 1913].

American Art Association. *Catalogue of an Unusual Collection of Water-color and Oil Paintings* (auction catalogue). New York: American Art Galleries, February 16–18, 1892.

Amherst College, Mead Art Gallery. *American Painters of the Arctic*. Amherst, Massachusetts, February 1–March 2, 1975.

Andersen, Timothy; Moore, Eudorah M.; and Winter, Robert W. (eds.). *California Design 1910*. Pasadena, California: California Design Publications, 1974. Exhibition at Pasadena Center, October 15–December 1, 1974.

Arkelian, Marjorie. *The Kahn Collection of Nineteenth-Century Paintings by Artists in California*. Oakland, California: The Oakland Museum, 1975.

Artists' Gallery. *Catalogue of the Valuable Collection of Paintings and Water Color Drawings of Messrs. Williams & Everett* (auction catalogue). Studio Building, Boston, May 2–3, 1872.

Baird, Joseph Armstrong, Jr. (comp.). *Catalogue of Original Paintings, Drawings and Watercolors in the Robert B. Honeyman, Jr. Collection*. Berkeley: The Friends of the Bancroft Library, University of California, 1968.

The Bohemian Club. *Exhibition of Paintings*. San Francisco, 1898.

Boston Art Club. Exhibition Catalogues. Boston, January, 1873; March, 1873; January 14–February 11, 1888.

Boston Athenaeum. *Catalogue of the Fiftieth Exhibition of Paintings*. Boston, July, 1873.

California Art Union. *A Classified Catalogue of the Paintings on Exhibition*. San Francisco, 1865.

California Arts Commission. *Horizons: A Century of California Landscape Painting*. Introduction by Keith E. Dennison. Sacramento, April, 1970–May, 1971 (traveling exhibition).

California Midwinter International Exposition. *Official Catalogue: Department of Fine Arts*. San Francisco, 1894.

California Pacific International Exposition. *Illustrated Catalogue: Official Art Exhibition of the California Pacific International Exposition*. Palace of Fine Arts, Balboa Park, San Diego, California, May 29–November 11, 1935.

California Palace of the Legion of Honor. *American Paintings of the Nineteenth Century*. San Francisco, July 4–August 16, 1964.

Catalogue of Leland Stanford's Collection of Pictures. San Francisco, 1882.

Catalogue of Louis Prang's Collection of Oil and Water-color Paintings. Public auction and exhibition, Copley Hall, Boston, November 23–December 8, 1899.

Catalogue of the Paintings and Sketches by the Late Thomas Hill. Robert R. Hill, Administrator. Exhibition Gallery, San Francisco, [December, 1910].

The Columbia Museum of Art. *Americana: A painting survey of the American scene from the collection of the C. Thomas May, Jr. family, Dallas, Texas*. Columbia, South Carolina, January 29–March 14, 1976.

E.B. Crocker Art Gallery. *Catalog of the E.B. Crocker Art Gallery*. Sacramento, 1928.

————. *Handbook*. Sacramento, 1937.

————. *Catalogue of Collections*. Sacramento, 1964.

The Currier Gallery of Art. *American Paintings of the Nineteenth Century from the Collection of Morton C. Bradley*. Manchester, New Hampshire, April 12–May 27, 1962.

Curry, Larry. *The American West*. Foreword by Archibald Hanna. Los Angeles: The Viking Press, Inc. in association with the Los Angeles County Museum of Art, March 21–December 31, 1972.

The M.H. de Young Memorial Museum. San Francisco: Park Commission, 1921.

Elliot, Blakeslee & Noyes. *Catalogue of Fine Oil Paintings* (sale catalogue). Boston, April–May 6, 1873.

Executors Sale of the David Hewes Collection of Valuable and Historical Paintings by the Late Thomas Hill. 532 Sutter Street, San Francisco, November 27–December 9, 1916.

Ferbrache, Lewis. *The Dr. and Mrs. Bruce Friedman Collection*. San Francisco: California Historical Society, September 30–November 15, 1969.

Fort Worth Art Center. *19th Century Painters of the Southwest: A Loan Exhibition from the Collections of J.N. Bartfield and Edward Eberstadt & Sons*. Fort Worth, Texas, April 14–May 4, 1958.

Golden Gate International Exposition. *Art: Official Catalog*. Palace of Fine Arts, San Francisco, 1940.

Golden Gate Park Memorial Museum. *First Exhibition of Painting and Sculpture by California Artists*. San Francisco, 1915.

The Frank C. Havens Collection of Paintings from the Piedmont Gallery (auction catalogue). San Francisco, October 18–22, 1917.

Hirschl & Adler Galleries. *Selections from the Collection of Hirschl & Adler Galleries*. New York, Vol. VII (1965–1966).

Hotel Del Monte Art Gallery. *Catalogue*. Del Monte, California, 1910–1911.

Huntington Galleries. *American Art: From the Limners to The Eight*. Huntington, West Virginia, February 1–May 2, 1976.

Kende Galleries. *Fine Paintings from an Eastern and North Western Museum and Private Collections*. New York, February 25–March 1, 1947.

The Longwood Fine Arts Center. *The American West: Selected Works from the Collection of Arthur J. Phelan, Jr.* Farmville, Virginia: Bedford Gallery, Longwood College, February 19–March 15, 1979.

Martin, Jean. *Louis Sloss, Jr. Collection of California Paintings*. San Francisco: California Historical Society, April–May, 1958.

Marzio, Peter C. *The Democratic Art: An Exhibition on the History of Chromolithography in America, 1840–1900*. Fort Worth, Texas: Amon Carter Museum of Western Art, September 6, 1979–September 28, 1980 (traveling exhibition).

Massachusetts Charitable Mechanic Association. *Catalogue of Paintings, Water-Colors, Engravings, Sculpture*. Boston, 1874.

Maxwell Galleries, Ltd. *Paintings of California*. San Francisco, March 5–31, 1962.

_____. *One Hundred Years of California Painting from 1849*. San Francisco, March 4–26, 1966.

Mills, Paul C. *Early Paintings of California in the Robert B. Honeyman, Jr. Collection*. Oakland, California: Oakland Art Museum, 1956.

_____. *"The Painted Flower:" An Exhibition of Floral Paintings in the Collection of Mr. and Mrs. Herbert Mortimer Stoll, Jr.* Oakland, California: Oakland Art Museum, May, 1957.

_____. *California Pictorial 1800–1900*. Santa Barbara, California: Santa Barbara Museum of Art, August 9–September 9, 1962.

_____. *Treasures from East Bay Collections*. Oakland, California: Oakland Art Museum, November, 1962.

_____. *The California Collection of William and Zelma Bowser*. Oakland, California: The Oakland Museum, May 26–September 27, 1970.

New-York Historical Society. *Catalogue of the New-York Historical Society*. New York: Printed for the Society, 1903.

The North Conway Library Association. *A Century of Art in the White Mountains*. North Conway, New Hampshire, July 11–17, 1965.

Noyes & Blakeslee Gallery. *Catalogue of Valuable Paintings of The Modern School of Art*. Boston, March 11–12, 1885.

Official Catalogue of the United States International Exhibition. Philadelphia: John R. Nagle & Company, 1876.

F.D. Osgood, Son & Co. *Catalogue of Modern Oil Paintings* (auction catalogue). Boston, April 11–13, 1876.

Panama-Pacific International Exposition. *Illustrated Official Catalogue of the Department of Fine Arts*. San Francisco: The Wahlgreen Company, 1915.

The Pennsylvania Academy of the Fine Arts. *Catalogue of the Sixty-sixth Annual Exhibition*. Philadelphia, December 21, 1896–February 22, 1897.

Rathbone, Perry T. *Charles Wimar, Painter of the Indian Frontier*. St. Louis, Missouri: City Art Museum of St. Louis, October 13–November 18, 1946.

St. Mary's College, Hearst Art Gallery. *A Half-Century of Collecting: Selections from the St. Mary's College Collection*. Moraga, California, October 9–December 14, 1977.

San Francisco Art Association. Exhibition Catalogues. San Francisco, 1872–1903.

Seavey, Kent L. *Artist-Teachers & Pupils: San Francisco Art Association and California School of Design, the First Fifty Years 1871–1921*. San Francisco: California Historical Society, June 1–September 4, 1971.

A Selection of American Paintings by Artists of the 19th Century Working in Northern California. Foreword by Charles Lindstrom. Sonoma, California: Mission San Francisco Solano de Sonoma, July, 1976.

Snow & Roos Art Gallery. *Catalogue of Pictures on Exhibition*. San Francisco, April, 1869.

The Society of California Pioneers. *Annual Publication for the Year 1955*. San Francisco, 1956.

Trask, John E.D. and Laurvik, J. Nilsen (eds.). *Catalogue de Luxe of the Department of Fine Arts, Panama-Pacific International Exposition*. 2 vols. San Francisco: Paul Elder and Company, 1915.

Truettner, William H. and Bolton-Smith, Robin. *National Parks and the American Landscape*. Foreword by Joshua C. Taylor. Washington, D.C.: The Smithsonian Institution Press, June 23–August 27, 1972.

University Art Museum. *Selection 1966: The University Art Collections*. Foreword by Peter Selz. Berkeley: University of California, May 20–September 9, 1966.

University of California, Davis. *From Frontier to Fire: California Painting from 1816 to 1906*. Davis, California, May 22–June 2, 1964.

University of Southern California Art Galleries. *Pack-in Painters of the American West*. Los Angeles, November 22–December 23, 1976.

Washington State University Museum of Art. *Artist and Place: American Landscape Painting, 1860-1914*. Pullman, Washington, May, 1977–April 6, 1978.

Woodward, Arthur and Byrnes, James B. *California Centennials Exhibition of Art*. Los Angeles: Los Angeles County Museum, September 30–November 13, 1949.

Newspapers

Alta California (San Francisco): October 5, 1864; March 27, 1870; April 3, 1870; January 28, 1873; April 20, 1874; January 8, 1875; January 22, 1875; January 28, 1875; November 7, 1875; April 15, 1877; April 19, 1877; July 1, 1877; October 18, 1877; December 19, 1878; January 29, 1881; March 23, 1881.

Bee (Sacramento): September 17, 1883; September 21, 1885; November 3, 1945; March 5, 1949; February 10, 1956.

Bulletin (San Francisco): September 8, 1864; February 10, 1871; October 16, 1872; November 14, 1872; November 23, 1872; November 26, 1872; December 6, 1872; December 10, 1873; February 5, 1874; April 2, 1874; April 4, 1874; April 11, 1874; March 27, 1875; May 1, 1875; June 15, 1875; September 4, 1875; March 6, 1879; March 1, 1880; March 4, 1880; July 16, 1899.

Call (San Francisco): December 6, 1872; January 27, 1880; April 25, 1880; March 10, 1882; December 12, 1882; April 28, 1885; December 22, 1886; May 28, 1893; December 1, 1893; September 9, 1906; July 11, 1909; July 15, 1909; November 14, 1910; November 27, 1910; December 8, 1910.

Call and Post (San Francisco), March 5, 1923.

Chronicle (San Francisco): November 15, 1872; December 6, 1872; December 12, 1873; February 6, 1874; November 8, 1874; January 14, 1877; February 11, 1877; April 5, 1877; April 22, 1877; June 3, 1877; December 8, 1879; April 4, 1880; May 9, 1880; October 3, 1880; March 23, 1881; April 3, 1881; February 18, 1883; December 28, 1883; December 29, 1883; October 4, 1891; January 8, 1893; January 11, 1896; October 8, 1899; July 2, 1908; August 29, 1915; December 3, 1916; March 24, 1917; March 25, 1917; October 21, 1917; December 4, 1932; April 1,

1938; October 7, 1941; October 22, 1951; December 15, 1961; March 3, 1966; March 10, 1966.

Commonwealth (Boston), June 15, 1872.

Elevator (San Francisco), July 21, 1865.

Examiner (San Francisco): November 10, 1874; January 16, 1880; November 28, 1880; March 22, 1881; November 1, 1913; November 21, 1913; November 29, 1913; January 14, 1916; September 9, 1977.

Gardner News (Gardner, Massachusetts), January 13, 1960.

Herald (Boston): May 25, 1884; September 29, 1929.

Jewish Times (San Francisco): March 5, 1880; March 12, 1880.

Los Angeles Times: April 19, 1913; November 30, 1939.

Marin Journal (San Rafael, California), June 7, 1877.

Mechanics' Fair Daily (San Francisco), August 17, 1882.

Mexican Herald, December 25, 1899.

Post (Boston), June 13, 1868.

Post (San Francisco): July 24, 1872; October 16, 1872; October 29, 1872; December 30, 1872; December 9, 1873; December 10, 1873; November 26, 1875; April 13, 1876; May 1, 1880; March 22, 1881; May 1, 1886.

Record-Union (Sacramento): August 19, 1879; September 17, 1886; September 19, 1890.

Star (New York), July 11, 1889.

Times (Palo Alto, California): November 14, 1910; March 20, 1965.

Transcript (Boston): January 27, 1868; February 24, 1868; February 28, 1868; March 18, 1868; April 23, 1868; June 13, 1868; June 17, 1868; November 3, 1868; November 5, 1868; November 10, 1868; November 13, 1868; November 25, 1868; November 30, 1868; December 3, 1868; December 9, 1868; November 22, 1870; December 1, 1870; December 7, 1870; July 2, 1908; March 25, 1914; November 21, 1914; November 28, 1923.

Tribune (Oakland, California): October 29, 1916; May 1, 1952; February 8, 1959; February 22, 1959; May 10, 1959; March 15, 1961; May 28, 1961; April 17, 1962.

Union (Sacramento): July 2, 1908; September 21, 1930; May 23, 1937; March 10, 1938; September 24, 1939; December 5, 1939.

White Mountain Echo (Bethlehem, New Hampshire): July 30, 1881; August 27, 1881; August 7, 1886; August, 1892.

Fig. 32: IRRIGATING AT STRAWBERRY FARM
12½ × 19 in.
Collection of The Bancroft Library
Honeyman Collection.

Periodicals and Articles

Anchorage Historical and Fine Arts Museum. *Newsletter*, December, 1976.

Antiques: LXXII:3 (September, 1957); LXXXVI:5 (November, 1964); CII:1 (July, 1972); CIII:1 (January, 1973); CIII:3 (March, 1973); CIV:2 (August, 1973); CIV:3 (September, 1973); CVII:1 (February, 1975); CX:2 (August, 1976); CX:6 (December, 1976); CXI:2 (February, 1977); CXI:4 (April, 1977); CXII:5 (November, 1977); CXIII:2 (February, 1978); CXIII:4 (April, 1978).

Argonaut (San Francisco): January 29, 1881; March 26, 1881; July 15, 1882; August 23, 1884; December 13, 1884; December 12, 1908.

Arkelian, Marjorie. "Background of a Painting: Muir Glacier, Alaska." *Art* (The Oakland Museum), VI:3 (May–June, 1978).

Art in America, LII:5 (October, 1964).

Bell, Irving. "They Painted Hills." *Historic New Hampshire* (Concord: New Hampshire Historical Society), II:1 (February, 1946).

Brainard, Charles H. "The Early Home of Whittier." *The Ramrod* (Haverhill, Massachusetts and Dover, New Hampshire), June, 1869. Reprinted from *New York Independent*.

California Art Gallery (San Francisco): I:1 (January, 1873); I:2 (February, 1873); I:3 (March, 1873); I:4 (April, 1873); I:5 (May, 1873); I:7 (July, 1873).

California Historical Society Notes (San Francisco): XIX:1 (January, 1967); XXII:5 (May, 1970).

California Historical Society Quarterly (San Francisco): III:4 (December, 1924); XXIV:3 (September, 1945); XXX:2 (June, 1951); XXXVII:1 (March, 1958).

Californian (San Francisco), V:27 (March, 1882).

Colby, William E. (ed.). "Notes and Correspondence." *Sierra Club Bulletin* (San Francisco), X:3 (1918).

Downes, William Howe. "American Painters of Mountains." *American Magazine of Art*, XXV:4 (October, 1932).

George, Hardy. "Thomas Hill's *Driving of the Last Spike*, A Painting Commemorating the Completion of America's Transcontinental Railroad." *Art Quarterly*, XXVII:1 (Spring, 1964).

Godfrey, Elizabeth H. "Thumbnail Sketches of Yosemite Artists: Thomas Hill." *Yosemite Nature Notes* (Yosemite: Yosemite Natural History Association), XXIII:3 (March, 1944).

Grizzly Bear (Los Angeles), III:5 (September, 1908).

Hunt, Rockwell D. (ed.). *California and Californians*. Vol. IV. Chicago: The Lewis Publishing Co., 1932.

Huth, Hans. "Yosemite: The Story of an Idea." *Sierra Club Bulletin* (San Francisco), XXXIII:3 (March, 1948).

Idler (North Conway, New Hampshire), 1880.

Jones, Idwal. "California's Controversial Painting." *Westways* (Los Angeles: Automobile Club of Southern California), XLIX:6 (June, 1957).

Kennedy Quarterly (New York: Kennedy Galleries, Inc.): III:2 (October, 1962); V:1 (October, 1964); V:3 (May, 1965); XI:2 (November, 1971); XII:3 (June, 1973); XII:4 (December, 1973); XIII:2 (June, 1974); IX:1 (June, 1969).

News Letter and California Advertiser (San Francisco): March 25, 1871; June 29, 1872; September 13, 1873; November 1, 1873; July 24, 1875; May 15, 1875; November 27, 1875; January 1, 1876; January 15, 1876; February 2, 1876; February 5, 1876; April 1, 1876; May 27, 1876; November 25, 1876; January 27, 1877; November 15, 1879; January 29, 1881; February 5, 1881; February 12, 1881; March 4, 1882; July 28, 1883.

Old Print Shop Portfolio (New York: The Old Print Shop): XXII:2 (October, 1962); XXII:5 (January, 1963); XXVIII:8 (April, 1969); XXIX:7 (March, 1970).

Overland Monthly (San Francisco): I:2 (August, 1868); XI:5 (November, 1873); XII:1 (January, 1874); XII:2 (February, 1874); XII:3 (March, 1874); XII:4 (April, 1874); XIII:5 (November, 1874); XIII:6 (December, 1874); XIV:1 (January, 1875); XIV:2 (February, 1875); XIV:3 (March, 1875); XIV:4 (April, 1875); XIV:6 (June, 1875); XV:1 (July, 1875); IX:51 (new series—March, 1887).

Pacific Coast Annual Mining Review and Stock Ledger (San Francisco), October, 1878.

Piazzoni, Gottardo. "Three Pioneer Artists." *Argus* (San Francisco), III:6 (September, 1928).

Roden, Anne R. "Special Exhibition in Gallery Eight." *Gilcrease Gazette* (Tulsa, Oklahoma: Thomas Gilcrease Institute of American History and Art), XVI:1 (January, 1978).

San Franciscan, January 31, 1885.

Sargent, Shirley. "Wawona's Yesterdays." *Yosemite Nature Notes* (Yosemite: Yosemite Natural History Association), XL:4 (November, 1961).

Stein, Louise. "Thomas Hill." *Artists of the Rockies and the Golden West*, VI:1 (Winter, 1979).

Wasp (San Francisco): May 10, 1886; December 23, 1911; March 29, 1913.

Wave (San Francisco), January 21, 1893.

Correspondence

Cederholm, Theresa D. (Boston Public Library) to Marjorie Arkelian (The Oakland Museum), April 4, 1979.

Coker, John (Birmingham, England) to Charles Smith (Piedmont, California), March 14, 1969. Courtesy of Mr. and Mrs. Charles C. Smith.

Greene, Phyllis F. (North Conway, New Hampshire) to Rudolph Wunderlich (Kennedy Galleries, New York), August 5, 1969.

_____. Letter to Marjorie Arkelian, July 16, 1979.

Hamlyn, Robin (The Tate Gallery, London) to Marjorie Arkelian, March 3, 1980.

Hartwig, Wawona Washburn (Beverly Hills, California) to Marjorie Arkelian, September 18, 1978; May 3, 1979.

Hill Family Letters, 1844–1861. Courtesy of Mr. and Mrs. Howard Lea and Mr. and Mrs. Charles C. Smith.

Hill, Benjamin (East Boston, Massachusetts) to "Dear Father and Mother" (England), April 13, 1861.

Hill, Mrs. C.W. (Oakland, California) to Mabel R. Gillis (California State Library), February, 1940. Courtesy of California State Library, Sacramento.

Hill, Robert R. (San Francisco) to Director of the School of Design, Mark Hopkins Institute of Art (San Francisco), December 14, 1910.

Hill, Thomas (tailor—New York) to Edward Kidd (Birmingham, England), October 8, 1843.

_____ (Taunton, Massachusetts) to Francis Hill (Wolverhampton, England), August 25, 1844.

_____ (Taunton) to "Dear Brother" (England), April 25, 1847.

Hill, Thomas (San Francisco) to John Muir, March 4, 1888. Courtesy of The Holt-Atherton Pacific Center for Western Studies, University of the Pacific, Stockton, California.

_____ (San Francisco) to Leland Stanford, November 22, 1889. Courtesy of Theodore Baggelmann.

_____ (Wawona, California) to John Odiorne, May 21, 1900. Courtesy of Mrs. Donald Wood.

_____ (Wawona) to Henry C. Peterson (Stanford University, Stanford, California), August 30, 1905. Courtesy of California State Library.

_____ (Wawona) to Henry C. Peterson, September 11, 1905. Courtesy of California State Library.

_____ (Wawona) to Henry C. Peterson, September 28, 1905. Courtesy of California State Library.

_____ (Raymond, California) to Henry C. Peterson (Palo Alto, California), January 12, 1906. Courtesy of California State Library.

_____ (Raymond) to Henry C. Peterson, February 18, [1906]. Courtesy of California State Library.

Jackson, Jack (Boston Athenaeum) to George W. Neubert (The Oakland Museum), May 24, 1979.

Kendall, Mrs. Stanley G. (Gardner, Massachusetts) to Charles C. Smith (Piedmont, California), n. d. Courtesy of Mr. and Mrs. Charles C. Smith.

Laing, Gregory H. (Haverhill Public Library, Haverhill, Massachusetts) to Marjorie Arkelian, May 23, 1979.

Lee, Dorothy McCullough (Portland, Oregon) to Marjorie Arkelian, August 27, 1979.

Mills, William H. (Central Pacific Railway Co., San Francisco) to Thomas Hill, January 24, 1902. Courtesy of Theodore Baggelmann.

Osborne, Carol M. (Stanford University Museum of Art, Stanford, California) to Marjorie Arkelian, December 3, 1979.

Peterson, Henry C. to Thomas Hill (Wawona), September 4, 1905. Courtesy of California State Library.

Robinson, Edward K. (South Dartmouth, Massachusetts) to Jane Cayford (New Hampshire Historical Society, Concord), January 7, 1963. Courtesy of New Hampshire Historical Society.

Spencer, Frs. E. to Thomas Hill (San Francisco), January 9, 1895. Courtesy of Theodore Baggelmann.

————— (San Jose, California) to Thomas Hill (Coronado Beach, California), January 26, 1895. Courtesy of Theodore Baggelmann.

Stover, Catherine (Pennsylvania Academy of the Fine Arts, Philadelphia) to Marjorie Arkelian, March 29, 1979.

Vogel, Charles (Townsend Harbor, Massachusetts) to Marjorie Arkelian, October 1, 1978.

—————. Letter to Barbara Bowman (The Oakland Museum), June 20, 1980.

Ward, Catherine (Lexington, Massachusetts) to Marjorie Arkelian, June 18, 1979; August 20, 1979.

Miscellaneous

Abajian, James de T. California Artists Card Catalogue. San Francisco, 1969–1979.

Alameda County, California. Office of Recorder. Records for Thomas and Charlotte M. Hill. Alameda County Courthouse, Oakland, California.

Alameda County, California. Superior Court. *Petition: Thomas Hill.* Alameda County Courthouse, Oakland, California, August 3, 1903.

Arkelian, Marjorie. "Descendents of John and Jane Hill" (genealogical chart). Archives of California Art, The Oakland Museum.

Bowman, Barbara. "Attack on the Emigrant Train" (research report). Archives of California Art, The Oakland Museum, 1980.

Bradshaw, Ysabel. "Thomas Hill" (The Kahn Collection research report). Archives of California Art, The Oakland Museum, 1969.

Norton Bush Scrapbook. Archives of California Art, The Oakland Museum.

Benjamin Champney Memorabilia. Information courtesy of Phyllis F. Greene.

Comstock, Sophia P. "Painters of Northern California." Part I. Lecture read before the Kingsley Art Club, Sacramento, California, March 15, 1909.

Conway House Register, 1859–1869. Conway, New Hampshire. Information courtesy of Phyllis F. Greene.

Edwin Deakin Scrapbook. Archives of California Art, The Oakland Museum.

"Early California Artists" (notebook). Collection of Frederick H. Meyer. Archives of California Art, The Oakland Museum, gift of Miss Laetitia Meyer, 1962.

Farquhar, Francis P. "Notes on Artists of the Sierra" (scrapbook). Archives of California Art, The Oakland Museum.

Fletcher, Robert H. *Memorandum of Artists*, 1906. California Section, California State Library, Sacramento.

George, Hardy Sloan. "Thomas Hill (1829–1908)." Master's thesis, University of California, Los Angeles, 1963.

Hanna, Richard R. Interviewed by George W. Neubert and Marjorie Arkelian, December 16, 1977.

Heywood-Wakefield Company. "Invitation to Market." Chicago, July 6–24, 1926. Archives of California Art, The Oakland Museum, gift of Cherene Holsinger and James W. Cravagan III, 1977.

Hill, Adeline Matilda. Interviewed (mail questionnaire) by Theodore Baggelmann, August, 1941.

Hill, Ethel. Interviewed by Ann Bernauer and Fredericka May, September 26, 1978. Archives of California Art, The Oakland Museum.

Hill Family Archives. Courtesy of Mr. and Mrs. Charles C. Smith, 1979.

Hill, Thomas (tailor). "Memorandum of the Ages of my Self and Brothers." Courtesy of Mr. and Mrs. Charles C. Smith.

Thomas Hill Memorabilia. Archives of California Art, The Oakland Museum, gift of Cherene Holsinger and James W. Cravagan III, 1977.

The Thomas Hill Studio Collection. Courtesy of Theodore Baggelmann.

Hill, Thomas. *History of the 'Spike Picture,' and why it is Still in my Possession.* Privately printed by Thomas Hill, 1884.

Hill, Thomas (attributed). *"The Last Spike," A Painting by Thomas Hill.* Printed by E. Bosqui & Co., San Francisco, January, 1881. Archives of California Art, The Oakland Museum, gift of Cherene Holsinger and James W. Cravagan III, 1977.

Hill, Thomas Virgil Troyon. "Remarks in Fathers letters to me" (memorandum book), n. d. Archives of California Art, The Oakland Museum, gift of Cherene Holsinger and James W. Cravagan III, 1977.

McCullough, Flora Hill. "Memoirs." Archives of California Art, The Oakland Museum, 1962.

————. "Memories of My Father: Thomas Hill—Artist of Yosemite," *Yosemite: Saga of a Century, 1864-1964.* Oakhurst, California: Sierra Star Press, 1964.

McGlynn, Betty Hoag. California Artists Research Collection, 1979.

Mariposa County, California. Superior Court. *Inventory and Appraisement for the Estate of Thomas Hill.* Mariposa, California, September 15, 1908.

May, Fredericka. "Muir Glacier" (research report). Archives of California Art, The Oakland Museum, 1978.

Mechanics' Institute and Library of San Francisco. *Industrial Exhibition Reports.* San Francisco, 1864, 1871, 1874–1889, 1894.

Mills, Paul C. Unpublished manuscript. Archives of California Art, The Oakland Museum, 1967.

National Collection of Fine Arts, Smithsonian Institution. "Inventory of American Paintings: Artist Index." Washington, D.C., 1977.

Oakland Art Museum. "The Nixon Collection" (exhibition mailer). Oakland, California, October 6–28, 1962.

Perret, Ferdinand. "The California Section of the Ferdinand Perret Research Library of the Arts and Affiliated Sciences" (card catalogue). Compiled in Los Angeles, 1936–1942.

Philadelphia City Archives. Records for United States Centennial Commission, International Exhibition, Pennsylvania, 1876.

Pioneer Records for Thomas Hill, February, 1940. California State Library, Sacramento.

San Francisco Art Association. Minutes of Board of Directors, March 21, 1871–August 29, 1889.

————. Minutes of the Committee of the School of Design, December 21, 1886.

"Smethcott" (Victoria Survey), *A County History of Shropshire,* n. d. Courtesy of Mr. and Mrs. Howard F. Lea and Mr. and Mrs. Charles C. Smith.

Stanford University Archives. "The Gold Spike." Stanford, California, rev. 1977.

Transactions of the California State Agricultural Society. Sacramento, 1879, 1881, 1886.

Wright, Marjorie. "Officers and Teachers of the San Francisco Art Association, 1871–1967" (research report). Archives of California Art, The Oakland Museum.

Catalogue of Thomas Hill Works in the Permanent Collection of The Oakland Museum

All paintings are oil on canvas, unless otherwise indicated.
Dimensions are in inches, followed by centimeters; height
precedes width.
Symbols defining the location of inscriptions are:

    (LL) lower left
    (LR) lower right

YOSEMITE (NORTH DOME AND GLACIER POINT,
YOSEMITE VALLEY)
Oil on cardboard
14 × 10½ (35.56 × 26.67)
Unsigned
Gift of Mr. and Mrs. James A. Hutzler (53.140)

SKETCH FROM NATURE, SUGAR PINES, YOSEMITE
VALLEY, 1875
Oil on cardboard
14⅜ × 10⅜ (36.51 × 26.35)
Signed (LR): T. Hill 75
Gift of anonymous donor (53.141)

WOODED STREAM
Oil on panel
22 × 14 (55.88 × 35.56)
Signed (LL): T. Hill
Gift of anonymous donor (55.4)

VIRGIL WILLIAMS' CABIN NEAR ST. HELENA (fig. 29)
14¾ × 22¼ (37.47 × 56.52)
Signed (LL): T. Hill
Gift of Mrs. Samuel Kahn and Mrs. Walter Mayer in memory of
their parents, Joseph and Harriet Weissbein (58.12)

VERNAL FALL, YOSEMITE, 1902
30 × 20 (76.20 × 50.80)
Signed (LR): T. Hill 1902
Gift of Mrs. H.H. Mitten (58.58.1)

A VILLAGE HOLIDAY OF THE OLDEN TIME:
"WHEN THE MERRY BELLS RING AROUND," 1858
(Copy of engraving by J. Carter taken from 1847 painting
by Frederick Goodall)
40 × 60½ (101.60 × 153.67)
Signed (LL): T. Hill 1858
Bequest of Miss Mary Elizabeth Fletcher (58.119.1)

SAN MATEO MARSHES AND DUCKS
14 × 30 (35.56 × 76.20)
Signed (LR): T. Hill
Gift of Mr. and Mrs. Howard Willoughby (60.33.6)

BRIDAL VEIL FALL, YOSEMITE VALLEY, 1892
53 × 35 (134.62 × 88.90)
Signed (LR): T. Hill 1892
Gift of Mrs. Leon Bocqueraz (61.5.1)

YOSEMITE VALLEY, 1889
53½ × 35 (135.89 × 88.90)
Signed (LR): T. Hill 1889
Gift of Mr. Fred Maxwell (61.30)

YOSEMITE FALLS
60½ × 36 (153.67 × 91.44)
Signed (LR): T. Hill
Bequest of Dr. Cecil E. Nixon (62.25.6)

YOSEMITE VALLEY FROM VICINITY OF INSPIRATION POINT
60 × 36 (152.40 × 91.44)
Signed (LR): T. Hill
Bequest of Dr. Cecil E. Nixon (62.25.7)

YOSEMITE VALLEY (EL CAPITAN AND BRIDAL VEIL FALL) (cover illus.)
88 × 72 (223.52 × 182.88)
Signed (LR): T. Hill
Bequest of Dr. Cecil E. Nixon (62.25.8)

LANDSCAPE (OLD ROAD TO YOSEMITE)
Oil on cardboard mounted on board
12 × 18 (30.48 × 45.72)
Signed (LR): T. Hill
Gift of Mr. and Mrs. Howard Willoughby (62.101.15)

LANDSCAPE (FOREST STREAM WITH FISHERMAN)
18 × 14⅛ (45.72 × 35.88)
Signed (LL): T. Hill
Gift of Mrs. Agnes Taylor Galbraith (64.27.3)

YOSEMITE VALLEY (FROM INSPIRATION POINT), 1890
26¾ × 34 (67.95 × 86.36)
Signed (LR): T. Hill 1890
Gift of Dr. and Mrs. Edward G. Ewer (64.37)

LAND'S END (fig. 2)
Oil on canvas mounted on masonite
15⅛ × 22 (38.42 × 55.88)
Signed (LR): T. Hill
Gift of Grace Decker Meyer in memory of her husband, Victorien Melville Meyer (65.24)

OUR CAMP (fig. 30)
12 × 18 (30.48 × 45.72)
Signed (LR): T. Hill
Gift of the Kahn Foundation (65.151)

FLOWERS IN A WINDOW (fig. 25)
36 × 20 (91.44 × 50.80)
Signed (LL): T. Hill
Gift of the Kahn Foundation (65.152)

VERNAL FALL, YOSEMITE
24 × 18 (60.96 × 45.72)
Signed (LR): T. Hill
Bequest of Louisiana Scott Shuman (66.23.1)

CALIFORNIA QUAIL, 1881 (fig. 15)
Oil on panel mounted on cardboard
13⅝ × 20¾ (34.61 × 52.71)
Signed (LR): T. Hill 1881
Gift of the Kahn Foundation (66.36)

PORTRAIT OF ALBERT SAMUEL LOZIER (1842–1894), [*ca.* 1872]
30 × 25 (76.20 × 63.50)
Unsigned
Gift of Miss Aimee Lozier (67.93.2)

PORTRAIT OF ANNETTE LEE (MRS. ALBERT SAMUEL) LOZIER
24 × 20¼ (60.96 × 51.44)
Unsigned
Gift of Miss Aimee Lozier (67.93.3)

YOSEMITE, INDIANS ON TRAIL
35⅜ × 26½ (89.85 × 67.31)
Unsigned
Gift of Mr. and Mrs. Stuart Cundell Kierulff (67.139)

YOSEMITE, TWO TROUT FISHERMEN
35⅜ × 26½ (89.85 × 67.31)
Unsigned
Gift of Mr. and Mrs. Stuart Cundell Kierulff (68.22)

LANDSCAPE, 1902
35 × 52¾ (88.90 × 133.99) (sight)
Signed (LR): T. Hill 1902
Gift of Mr. Alan Field (68.131)

YOSEMITE VALLEY (FROM BELOW SENTINEL DOME, AS SEEN FROM ARTIST'S POINT), 1876 (fig. 11)
72 × 120 (182.88 × 304.80)
Signed (LR): T. Hill 1876
Gift of the Kahn Foundation (68.133.1)

MUIR GLACIER, ALASKA (fig. 21)
36 × 54¼ (91.44 × 137.80)
Signed (LL): T. Hill
Gift of Mr. and Mrs. Richard R. Hanna (78.18)

MEMORABILIA
Pencil sketches, photographs, artist's notes, etc.
Gift of Cherene Holsinger and James W. Cravagan III (77.158.1–40(1–4)

> CASTLE PEAKS NEAR MT. SHASTA (77.158.1)
> Pencil on paper
> 10¼ × 6⅞ (26.04 × 17.45)
> Inscription (bottom): Castle Peaks near Mt. Shasta/ Painted by Thomas Hill
>
> 11 SKETCHES FROM NATURE (77.158.3(1–12)
> Pencil on paper
> 3¾ × 5⅝ (9.53 × 14.29) each